SERVING THE BODY OF CHRIST

SERVING
THE BODY
OF CHRIST

The Magisterium
on Eucharist
and Ordained Priesthood

KEVIN W. IRWIN

Paulist Press
New York / Mahwah, NJ

Cover photos, clockwise from top left: by Lisa F. Young / Shutterstock.com; by Nano/iStockphoto.com; by Bob Denelzen / Shutterstock.com; by Steven Frame / Shutterstock.com; by FrankyDeMeyer/iStockphoto.com; by SW Productions / Mediabakery; by Pojoslaw/Shutterstock.com; by mangostock/Shutterstock.com; by Katrina Brown / Shutterstock.com; from Mediabakery

Cover design by Sharyn Banks
Book design by Lynn Else

Library of Congress Cataloging-in-Publication Data

Irwin, Kevin W.
    Serving the body of Christ : the Magisterium on Eucharist and ordained priesthood / Kevin W. Irwin.
        pages cm
    Includes bibliographical references.
    ISBN 978-0-8091-4850-9 (alk. paper) — ISBN 978-1-58768-318-3
        1. Mass. 2. Lord's Supper—Catholic Church. 3. Priesthood—Catholic Church. 4. Pastoral theology—Catholic Church. 5. Catholic Church—Doctrines. I. Title.
    BX2230.3.I795 2013
    234'.163 —dc23

                                                                            2013011455

ISBN: 978-0-8091-4850-9 (paperback)   ISBN: 978-1-58768-318-3 (e-book)

Published by Paulist Press
997 Macarthur Boulevard
Mahwah, New Jersey 07430

www.paulistpress.com

Printed and bound in the
United States of America

Contents

Dedicated to the Memory of
Rev. Patrick M. Carroll and Rev. Patrick D. Hennessy

Preface

I met the two Patricks to whom I dedicate this book in the fall of 1963 at Cathedral College in New York City. We were classmates and friends from then, through our ordination in 1971 in the Archdiocese of New York, and far beyond. As were all my classmates, we were assigned to parishes after ordination. My assignments took me to a rural parish, then to a suburban one, and then to further studies in Rome. Their assignments took them repeatedly to inner-city parishes where their mastery of the Spanish language and their love for a number of different ethnic populations taught me "multiculturalism" before I studied it. Even when my assignments took me away from the archdiocese for academic years abroad and to Washington, DC, we always reconnected on vacations. Their last visit to DC was to tour the then newly opened Holocaust Museum; it was typical of them to want to discover new places and learn new things, even though Pat Carroll was starting to show the signs of a debilitating illness. Some years later Pat Hennessy was diagnosed with cancer.

Both Patricks taught me a great deal about living and ministering. They also taught me a great deal about dying—patiently, valiantly, faithfully, lovingly, courageously. In the end what else could one ask of a friend but to be an example in life and in death? Not a day goes by that I do not remember them at the altar and in my prayers, thinking of how they lived what this book is about—the intrinsic relationship between Eucharist and ordained priesthood—and how they spent their lives for the people of God with all the variety that makes up the Catholic Church.

When we were ordained, the then new rite of ordination had just been put into use. We were among the first to hear the bishop say,

"May God who has begun this good work in you bring it to fulfillment" (adapted from the Letter to the Philippians 1:6). God began and completed a great work in and through them. In God's providence they have been taken from the earthly to the heavenly liturgy. May they continue to intercede for the rest of the class of 1971 from the Archdiocese of New York and for all priests who give their lives *serving the body of Christ*.

Introduction

Studying the Magisterium on Eucharist and Orders

What does the word *magisterium* mean?

In classical Latin, *magister* meant "master," not only in the sense of schoolmaster or teacher, but in the many ways one can be a "master" of an art, a craft, or a trade; hence the term carries the connotations of the role or the authority of one who is a master.

In modern Catholic usage, the term *magisterium* has come to be associated almost exclusively with the teaching role and authority of the hierarchy. Today, *magisterium* more commonly refers not only to the teachings themselves but also to those who exercise authority in teaching —namely, the pope and the bishops.[1]

That there has been a proliferation in the number of documents issued by modern popes and the Vatican is clear. But what is not always clear is their relative weight and the influence they should have.

A major strength of the Catholic theological tradition is the opportunity, not to say necessity, of making distinctions—for example, as St. Thomas Aquinas did in his *Summa*. An important principle in interpreting documents from the Vatican is to be aware of a document's "genre" and the relative importance the church assigns to that document precisely because of its genre. To assert that "the Vatican says..." may be a convenient way to introduce "breaking news" on any of a range of possible topics in documents and other sources; but it can be sloppy theologically and can ignore the fact that there is a clear and definitive "hierarchy" that the church itself assigns to its documents.[2]

HERMENEUTICS, OR INTERPRETATION

The scientific study of interpretation (in our present case, the interpretation of texts) is called "hermeneutics." Hermeneutics is the concern of this introduction. The more precise issue we need to consider is this: How can one determine the relative weight to be given to church documents where precision about *content* in the Catholic theological tradition always needs to be contextualized by an appreciation of the *genre* of a specific magisterial document? (I say this especially in a "blogosphere" Internet world in which issues of accuracy about what church sources actually say, as well as necessary distinctions about the genre of church documents, can easily be, not to say are often, lost.) I also do this, aware of the contemporary debates about the meaning and use of such terms as the "hermeneutic of continuity and discontinuity."[3]

Throughout this book I will analyze the data presented from official church sources, offer ideas about "unfinished business," and suggest additional avenues that might be explored from within our Catholic theological tradition to articulate a theology of the Eucharist and ordained priesthood—what that theology is and what it might be. I do this with the conviction that we are faithful to the Catholic theological tradition by just such reflection based on sources and using them as a basis to draw out additional possibilities. I judge that these reflections are a "work in progress," just as much as I judge any ministering in education, formation, and pastoral life as always "a work in progress."

Two methodological principles are often at work for me when it comes to magisterial documents.

1. *It is important to place texts in context.* Put simply, this means that the texts from the Council of Trent reflect the polemics and politics of the Reformation. The texts from Vatican II, while also emanating from a church council, do not reflect the same polemical era or document style in terms of condemnations. This means that levels of meaning can be uncovered by recalling the time and place in the church's life where and when a particular text was crafted.

2. *It is important to compare and contrast what a prior document and a subsequent document on the same subject asserted.* This is to examine whether a particular issue or phrasing of an issue perdures or is nuanced or in fact changes. Thus, we must be attentive to exactly what was said, when, and where.

In each of the chapters that deal with what the magisterium says about the Eucharist and ordained priesthood, I will begin by recalling some of the salient points from the Council of Trent's teachings about priestly ordination in that particular council's historical context. I then consider the documents of Vatican II and follow this with an examination of select, but what I judge to be representative, texts from the magisterium as official postconciliar church teaching. In each instance I will recall the nature of the document at hand.

I approach this topic as a trained (sacramental) theologian. In what follows, priority will be given to magisterial statements about Eucharist and ordained priesthood, especially the evolution of such statements from Trent to today—noting, in particular, important instances of continuity and change in the church's self-understanding of both. In what follows with regard to the Eucharist, I have been conscious of the need to express in a tandem relationship some ideas about a theology of real presence and sacrifice from Trent with a theology of the celebration of the eucharistic liturgy as expressed in the documents of Vatican II and since. With regard to the theology of ordained ministry, I have been conscious of the evolution in church documents from emphasizing a theology of the *ministers* to a theology of the *ministry itself* to which they are called and for which they are ordained.

As I begin I am well aware of the inherent complexity at stake in this project. In the Introduction to the bibliographical resource series entitled *Sacramenta*,[4] the editor, Maksimilijan Zitnik, indicates that he found an inherent "interdisciplinarity" involved in studying the sacraments, as well as in categorizing studies about them for his rich and important four-volume research tool. I found (and still find) myself reflecting on this word as I continued to research the phenomenon and theology of the Eucharist and the ordained priesthood today. The genesis of this book's section on magisterium was a study paper for the United Methodist–Roman Catholic dialogue in June 2010. And the genesis for the chapters on ordained priesthood was a paper delivered at an international meeting of Sulpician priests in Montreal in July 2012. And so, with interdisciplinarity in mind, I offer the results of that reflection and research in light of the documents of Vatican II, in light of their immediate predecessors in data from the decrees and canons from the Council of Trent, and in light of contemporary magisterial documents, including postsynodal exhortations, an encyclical, the *Catechism of the Catholic Church*, and so forth.

Among the allied and related issues that bear upon the Eucharist and ordained priesthood are ecclesiology, Christology, soteriology, pneumatology, and trinitarian studies. In addition, I am conscious of how the Eucharist is understood to be "the sacrament of sacraments," to which and from which all other sacraments are ordered, and the way the sacrament of orders/order relates to the theology of baptism and the theology of other ordained ministries. Closely allied with this issue of the interdisciplinarity of the theology of Eucharist and ordained priesthood are issues about spirituality, relating the Eucharist to daily life, priestly lifestyle, pastoral work, a life of virtue, and many others. Church documents say many important things. They do not and cannot say everything that can or should be said about a particular topic or issue, not to mention topics as central to church life as are Eucharist and ordination.

HIERARCHY OF DOCUMENTS

In what follows, pride of place will be given to the statements from Trent and Vatican II simply because, being the results of a council, they carry the highest theological weight. It is commonly held that among the "acts of the Holy See," as published in the Vatican's official organ *Acta Apostolicae Sedis* (Latin, starting in 1909), the highest rank is ascribed to the "acts of the Second Vatican Council." The same *Acta* publishes papal documents and pronouncements. After the "solemn profession of faith," it ranks "acts for the beginning and conclusion of the Second Vatican Council" as of highest authority, followed by such documents as "decretals," "encyclical letters," "apostolic exhortations," addresses to consistories, apostolic constitutions, the *motu proprio*, and other papal pronouncements.[5] What is less easy to define is the authoritative weight to be given to a postsynodal exhortation, given the comparatively recent appearance of this kind of document (recall that meetings of international synods began only after Vatican II, the first of which was held in Rome in 1967). While papal apostolic exhortations have traditionally been ranked after encyclicals and before apostolic letters "*motu proprio*," these postsynodal exhortations are not only signed by the pope but are also designed to explain and elaborate on the results of a synod of bishops; thus they are a distillation of the synodical process and an act of representatives of the whole episcopal college. This means that they merit greater weight than an apostolic exhortation signed by the pope without the input of the synod process.[6]

INTERPRETING THE DOCUMENTS OF VATICAN II

Because we have just commemorated the fiftieth anniversary of the summoning of the Second Vatican Council, I judge it important to say a word about the ongoing, necessary, and very fruitful debate about how to interpret the Council.

A distinction must be made among the "hierarchy" of the Council's documents—constitutions, decrees, and declarations, in that order. In what follows, therefore, priority will be given to the Constitution on the Sacred Liturgy (*Sacrosanctum Concilium*, the first Council document, promulgated in 1963) and to the Constitution on the Church (*Lumen Gentium*, promulgated in 1964). At the same time, just because a conciliar decree or declaration is not a constitution does not mean that it does not carry significant weight. For example, the Declaration of the Relationship of the Church to Non-Christian Religions (*Nostra Aetate*, promulgated in 1965) has come to be among the most important of the Council's texts for the ongoing commitment to the Catholic Church's relations with Jews and Muslims, largely under the influence of postconciliar papal leadership (for example, Pope John Paul II). Therefore, in what follows, especially regarding ordained priesthood, the Council's decrees on both priestly formation and the ministry and life of priests will be carefully addressed.

More particularly, my concern here will be to underscore the necessity for asserting as precisely as possible what was said in the documents given the context and content of the debates on the Council floor,[7] the subsequent revisions of the texts during the Council before their implementation, and something about their reception and ongoing implementation.[8]

I think it important to note that some of the present debates about a "hermeneutic of continuity" over against a "hermeneutic of discontinuity" really do not reflect precisely what Pope Benedict XVI said in his address to the members of the Roman Curia on December 22, 2005. In a central part of that address, referring to addresses of his predecessors Pope John XXIII and Paul VI, he stated:

> On the one hand, there is an interpretation that I would call "a hermeneutic of discontinuity and rupture"; it has frequently availed itself of the sympathies of the mass media, and also one trend of modern theology. On the other, there is the "hermeneutic of reform," of renewal in the continuity of the one subject-Church which the Lord has given to us. She is a subject which increases in time and develops, yet always remaining the same, the one subject of the journeying People of God.
>
> The hermeneutic of discontinuity risks ending in a split between the pre-conciliar Church and the post-conciliar Church. It asserts that the texts of the Council as such do not yet express the true spirit of the Council. It claims that they are the result of compromises in which, to reach unanimity, it was found necessary to keep and reconfirm many old things that are now pointless. However, the true spirit of the Council is not to be found in these compromises but instead in the impulses toward the new that are contained in the texts.[9]

It is not uncommon today to criticize "the Bologna School" of interpreting Vatican II—whose chief proponent was Giuseppe Alberigo and whose chief (and lasting) publishing contribution is his five-volume *History of Vatican II*—for upholding the hermeneutic of discontinuity.[10] My own sense is that its individual essays should stand alongside those in Herbert Vorgrimler's *Commentary on the Documents of Vatican II*[11] and that these should be seen as mutually enriching. In my judgment, each of these (monumental) commentaries offers a diachronic reading of each conciliar document based on careful historical reconstruction of the editing of the various *schemata* and summaries of the floor debates about the individual documents. In addition, in the Alberigo volumes there are some introductory stand-alone essays that are rich in theological depth based on the conciliar debates and the evolution of the Council itself.[12] What may have cast a shadow on these essays was the excision of various, more editorialized pieces from the five volumes written by Alberigo himself and published in one volume entitled *A Brief History of Vatican II*.[13] As the Council progressed, Alberigo detects a certain loss of nerve, a judgment that unfortunately has caused some to marginalize the important work of the Bologna School.

At the risk of oversimplifying and of focusing narrowly on Italian authors, I think it worth noting that the subtitle of Agostino Marchetto's *The Second Vatican Ecumenical Council* is *A Counterpoint for the History of the Council*,[14] since it has been observed that Marchetto aims to counterbalance the influence of the Bologna School of conciliar interpretation. Another counterpoint to the Bologna School's approach is Roberto De Mattei's *Il concilio Vaticano II*;[15] however, I am unable to recommend it due to its lack of balance and, in some places, lack of accuracy.

Still another Italian offering—what might be called an independent voice—is that of Massimo Faggioli in *Vatican II: The Battle for Meaning*.[16] In my opinion this book deserves wide readership for its assessment of the debates about how to interpret Vatican II. Faggioli's more recent book, *True Reform: Liturgy and Ecclesiology in Sacrosanctum Concilium*,[17] deserves equal attention.

Two English-speaking authors who have influenced my understanding of the documents of Vatican II are Ormond Rush (*Still Interpreting Vatican II*)[18] and Richard Gaillardetz (*The Church in the Making*).[19] I find the writings of John O'Malley, especially *What Happened at Vatican II*,[20] to be very useful, in particular for setting out the cultural and historical context for the Council. His more recent essay on the notion of "the hermeneutic of reform" lays out important historical and theological insight about Pope Benedict XVI's use of this concept as an interpretative key for Vatican II.[21]

Another aspect of the authority of a conciliar document (and most other church documents) is that the officially promulgated Latin text is the authorized text. In an Internet world, it is relatively easy to call up the Latin text of Vatican documents and their modern language translations.[22] Especially because we are two generations removed from the events of Vatican II, it is important to be very attentive about what the text says precisely and exactly in Latin. Years ago the eyewitnesses at Vatican II could have helped us interpret words and phrases in the documents, but this is simply not possible today.[23] The issue of translation of church documents has become a front-and-center concern in light of the revised edition of the Roman Missal. I still find wisdom in the Italian proverb, "Every translator is a traitor." As will be seen in the following chapters, I have been attentive to the Latin originals of the texts at hand and have taken the liberty of correcting some of the English translations of documents in light of the Latin originals.

Chapter One

What the Magisterium Says about the Eucharist

The documents to be reviewed here are from the canons, decrees, and teachings of the Council of Trent (1545–63); the encyclical *Mediator Dei* of Pius XII (1947); Vatican II's Constitution on the Sacred Liturgy (*Sacrosanctum Concilium*, 1963); the encyclical *Mysterium Fidei* of Paul VI (1965); selections from the *Catechism of the Catholic Church* (1992); the encyclical *Ecclesia de Eucharistia* of John Paul II (2003); the instruction *Redemptionis Sacramentum* (from the Congregation for Divine Worship (2004); the apostolic letter *Mane Nobiscum Domine* of John Paul II (2004);[1] the postsynodal apostolic exhortation *Sacramentum Caritatis* (2007); the apostolic letter (*motu proprio*) *Summorum Pontificum* (2007); the papal letter accompanying *Summorum Pontificum* (2007); and the postsynodal apostolic exhortation *Verbum Domini* (2010) by Benedict XVI.[2]

An operative principle in what follows is that, in order to understand the contents and import of a church document on a particular topic, it is helpful to place it in the context of what was said before it and after it in other church documents on the same topic.[3] Because an understanding of the ecclesial, liturgical, and theological background to a particular document is essential to understanding it correctly, this chapter will begin with a discussion of the normative and theologically binding canons and decrees from the Council of Trent on the Eucharist.[4]

DECREES, CANONS, AND TEACHINGS OF THE COUNCIL OF TRENT

Because of Trent's unique place in Western Christianity in the sixteenth century (politically, religiously, liturgically, and theologically),[5] and because of the way it framed subsequent teaching on the Eucharist in catechisms and in magisterial literature, it is important to review carefully the assertions of the Council of Trent and to appreciate what these assertions say and what they left unsaid about the Eucharist.

It is commonly accepted that the fathers at Trent did not intend in any way to lay out a complete theology of the Eucharist (or the ordained priesthood, or the sacraments in general). Rather, it is commonly agreed that at least four hermeneutical principles should be brought to bear on interpreting Trent's teachings: (1) Trent's decrees are *laconic*, in that precise words and terms are used that require careful interpretation; (2) they are *reactive to errors*, in that they address burning controversies of the time from a Roman Catholic (reactive) posture in order to correct contemporary misinterpretations; (3) they are *specific*, in that they concern the precise issues of what is contained in the sacrament (that is, presence) and what is the sacrificial nature of the Eucharist; and (4) they are *open-ended*, in that the decrees are not intended to limit theological descriptions of the Eucharist or its breadth and meaning in the life of the church.[6] At the same time, because they are the result of the deliberations of an ecumenical council, these assertions carry the highest theological weight and are understood to be operative and applicable to the church in whatever circumstance it finds itself.[7]

There are four decrees from Trent that concern the Eucharist specifically:[8] the Decree on the Most Holy Sacrament of the Eucharist (Session 13, October 1551); Communion under Two Species (Session 21, July 1562); the Teaching and Canons on the Most Holy Sacrifice of the Mass (Session 22, September 1562); and the Decree on Things to Be Observed and Avoided in Celebrating Mass (Session 22, September 1562). Because of their doctrinal focus, the first and third sets of decrees, about the holy sacrament and about sacrifice, are the most important for our purposes. The very fact that Trent devoted four decrees to the Eucharist itself is evidence of the importance they accorded to it. That the two more doctrinal decrees are separated by eleven years (The Most Holy Sacrament in 1551 and The Most Holy Sacrifice of the Mass in 1562) is at least notable. That the debates about the eucharistic sacrifice were protracted signaled how divisive this issue was in the sixteenth century.

A proper interpretation of Trent requires that we separate the decree (on the holy sacrament) and the teaching (on the sacrifice of the Mass), on the one hand—from the canons that follow, on the other. In effect, the canons contain what Catholics must believe; the prior sections of each chapter (decree and teaching) describe positively what the "anathema" ("let them be condemned")[9] statements contain. "The [whole] teaching of the chapter is definitive at least to the extent that it contradicts the anathema in the canon. But, besides containing defined doctrine, the decrees and teachings often contain additional explanatory matter that is not infallibly taught."[10]

DECREE ON THE MOST HOLY SACRAMENT
OF THE EUCHARIST[11]

In fact, the term *real presence* is found only once—in the chapter heading for chapter 1, "on the real presence of our Lord Jesus Christ in the most holy sacrament of the eucharist"—and the word *present* is used twice: "sacramentally present"[12] and "present" in the sacrament.[13] In two other places the verb used is "contained" in the sacrament.[14]

The canons of Trent on the sacrament make the following assertions.[15] That the body and blood of the Lord are contained "truly, really and substantially" (note it does not say "physically") in the sacrament. Notable toward the end of this paragraph is the assertion that "he is present [not] only as a sign or figure or by his power." Clearly the fathers wanted to avoid any prejudice against "sign," "figure" or "power," because these terms were consistently used in the patristic era to describe the Eucharist.[16] (It is notable that Pope Benedict XVI uses *figura* twice in his postsynodal exhortation *Sacramentum Caritatis*, numbers 9 to 11.) Then the decree asserts that the "unique change" in the Eucharist is of "the whole substance of bread" and "wine" into the body and blood, and that this change is "most aptly" called "transubstantiation." (The Latin here is *aptissime* for "most aptly" or "most fitting." It does not say that one must always and everywhere use the term *transubstantiation*.) It asserts that Christ is present after the consecration and not only "in its use," that Christ is present "sacramentally and really" (not "only spiritually"), that the holy sacrament is worthy of adoration, that it can be carried to the sick, that the priest may give communion to himself, that after the age of discretion one must receive the Eucharist at least once a year and that persons "burdened by an awareness of mortal sin" "must first avail themselves of sacramental confession" "granted the availability of a confessor."

The Decree on the Most Holy Sacrament of the Eucharist offers instructive theological amplification.[17] Its opening statement asserts directly that Trent intended to "supply a remedy for all the heresies and other serious troubles by which the church is now miserably disturbed and torn apart in a great variety of divisions, [and that one of its aims was] to tear up root and branch the tares of those detestable errors and schisms...in the teaching of faith in the most holy Eucharist and its use and liturgy." The decree then asserts (more positively) in chapter 1 that the Eucharist is "the very sacrament which the Savior left in his church as a symbol [*in ecclesia sua tanquam symbolum reliquit eius unitatis et caritatis*] of its unity and love whereby he wished all Christians to be mutually linked and united." It is notable that the term *symbol* is used, attesting to its importance as a term to describe liturgy and sacraments. Chapter 2 is perhaps the most theologically rich of the chapters in that it relates the Eucharist to memorial, eschatology, food, an antidote to free us from faults, the pledge of future glory, and the unity of the church. Chapter 3 speaks of the Eucharist as "a sign of a sacred reality and the visible form of invisible grace."[18] Chapter 4 asserts that "by the consecration of the bread and wine, there takes place the change of the whole substance of the bread into the whole substance of the body of Christ our Lord, and of the whole substance into the substance of his blood. And the holy Catholic Church has suitably and properly [*convenienter et proprie*] called this transubstantiation."

12

While chapter 5's title is "The Worship and Reverence to Be Shown to This Most Holy Sacrament," the assertion that introduces this presentation is important theologically. It states that the sacrament was "instituted by Christ the Lord in order to be consumed [*a Cristo domino, ut sumatur, institutum*]." That the Eucharist is regarded as for communion is significant, and this reiterates some of the more expressive language contained in chapter 2 (noted above). Interestingly, while the main assertion of chapter 6 is that the Eucharist should be reserved and can be taken to the sick, the word *adoration* or what practices ought to be connected with such reservation are absent. Chapter 7 concerns "the worthy reception of the holy Eucharist," and chapter 8 concerns "the use of this wonderful sacrament." In light of the preceding chapter (7), it is not surprising that chapter 8 makes the distinction between "sacramental" and "spiritual" communion, with the former reserved to those who judge themselves worthy.

TEACHING AND CANONS ON THE MOST HOLY SACRIFICE OF THE MASS[19]

The tersely worded canons (authoritative conciliar teachings) deal with some of the most theologically controversial issues that lay before Trent: the priesthood, the eucharistic offering, the propitiatory value of the Eucharist, and the sacrificial nature of the Eucharist.

From a theological perspective, it is very interesting that the first canon asserts, not that the Eucharist is a sacrifice, but that "a true and proper sacrifice is...offered to God in the Mass [*offerri Deo verum et proprium sacrificium*]." Thus the dynamism of the eucharistic action is underscored from the outset. The command "do this in memory of me" (again emphasizing enactment) is mentioned in chapter 2 to refer to the teaching that Christ did "make the apostles priests" and that "other priests should offer his body and blood [*instituisse apostolos sacerdotes, aut non ordinasse, ut ipsi aliique sacerdotes offerrent corpus et sanguinem suum*]." It is notable that the word *ordinasse* refers to what Christ intended, namely, that there be priests; it does not refer to their being *ordained* priests. Instead, the term *institute* is used. When chapter 3 asserts that the Mass is more than a sacrifice of praise and thanksgiv-

13

ing, it defers to the language of the by-then revered Roman Canon that uses *sacrificium laudis* and variations on it throughout this text. When it refers to the Mass as more than a commemoration, it defers to the language of both the Roman Canon and the Last Supper (already referred to above) where "do this in memory of me" recalls the language and reality of liturgical commemoration. One can legitimately infer that when the Canon asserts that the sacrifice is valuable for the sins and penalties of the living and the dead and that it aids in their satisfactions and other needs, this is based on the ecclesiology of eucharistic participation. These statements precede the assertion that the sacrifice of the Mass has "propitiatory" value (*autem propitiatorium*), that is to say that it is "appeasing."[20]

The heightened (polemical?) rhetoric of the time, which claimed that the eucharistic sacrifice is blasphemy, is directly countered in chapter 4. The intercessory value of the Mass is asserted in chapter 5, referring to the saints (again, one can infer that ecclesiology is operative here). Chapters 6 through 9 assert the value and doctrinal integrity of the rite of the Mass as celebrated and offer direct counterpoints to several contemporary critiques of the Mass: errors in texts, rubrics, vestments, priest as sole communicant, vernacular, two species, and so forth. Much of this is taken up again in the following Decree on Things to Be Observed and Avoided in Celebrating Mass.[21]

The issue of authority is asserted in the introduction to the "teaching" on sacrifice, which title begins the explanatory section (again, which precedes the canons). It asserts that "in order that the ancient faith and the great mystery of the Eucharist may be retained in the holy Catholic Church...the holy ecumenical and general council of Trent, lawfully assembled in the Holy Spirit, teaches and declares all that follows concerning the Eucharist...." (The very first words of the Latin state: "*Sacrosancta oecumenica et generalis Tridentina synodus in Spiritu sancto legitime congregata.*")[22] The next phrase is very important theologically because it asserts from the start that "the Eucharist...is a true and unique sacrifice," as opposed to a repeatable sacrifice. Further on, it asserts that our Lord "was to offer himself once to God the Father on the altar of the cross [*Deus et Dominus noster, etsi semel se ipsum in ara crucis, morte intercedente, Deo Parti onlaturus erat]*" and that he left "to his beloved spouse the Church a visible sacrifice (as human nature requires), by which that bloody sacrifice carried out on the cross should be represented, its memory persist until the end of time [*ut dilectae sponsae suae ecclesiae visibile (sicut hominum natura exigit) relinqueret sacrificium, quo cruentem illud semel in cruce peragendum repraesentaretur eiusque memoria in finem usque saeculi permaneret]*."[23]

Chapter 2 asserts that the Mass is the same sacrifice as that once offered by Christ: "in this divine sacrifice which is performed in the mass, the very same Christ is contained and offered in bloodless manner who made a bloody sacrifice of himself once for all on the cross [*in divino hoc sacrificio, quod in missa peragitur, idem ille Christus continentur et incruente immolatur, qui in ara crucis semel se ipsum cruente obtulit]*"; this is immediately followed by the assertion that the sacrifice is "truly propitiatory" (*"vere propitiatorium esse"*), that it is the same victim (*"hostia"*) "here offering himself by the ministry of his priests who then offered himself on the cross [*idem nunc offerens sacerdotium ministerio, qui se ipsum tunc in cruce obtulit]*."[24]

Chapter 3 declares that the sacrifice of the Mass is offered to God and not to the saints (*"non tamen illis sacrificium offerri docet, sed Deo soli"*).[25] The faithful are encouraged to "communicate in [the Eucharist] not only by spiritual devotion but also by sacramental reception [*non solum spirituali affectu, sed sacramentali etiam euchariatias perceptions communicarent]*" so that "the fruits of this sacrifice could be theirs more fully [*quo ad eos sanctissimi huius sacrificii fructus uberior proveniret]*."[26] This section helpfully ends with a reference to the ecclesiology of the Mass, namely, "to all the faithful who belong to the body of Christ [*qui ad corpus Christi pertinent]*." The (important) chapter on encouraging the explanation of the Mass to the faithful (*"aliquid exponat atque inter cetera sanctissimi huius sacrificii mysterium aliquod declarent..."*) asserts that "although the mass is full of instruction for the faithful people, the council fathers did not think that it should everywhere be celebrated in the vernacular [*etsi missa magnam contineat populi fidelis eruditionem, non tamen expedire visum est patribus, ut vulgari passim lingua celebraretur]*."[27]

In sum, it can be said that when Trent refers in this set of canons and decrees to the sacrificial nature of the Mass, it asserts that the Mass is a visible, propitiatory sacrifice. When it speaks of Christ's sacrifice, it most often uses variations on the expression *to offer* (*offere*). In the decree on observing what should be done in the celebration of the Mass, the text that refers to the priest's role employs the word *immolo* when it asserts that the life-giving victim is offered (*immolatur*) daily by priests in the Mass.[28] Neither the 1551 decree on the Eucharist nor this 1562 decree uses this word.[29]

MEDIATOR DEI—ENCYCLICAL OF POPE PIUS XII (1947)

We now switch magisterial genres from the canons of the ecumenical Council of Trent to a papal encyclical. With regard to the theological genre "encyclical" Avery Dulles asserts:

> Encyclical letters are normally addressed by the pope to the entire episcopate or the entire world. Encyclicals have rarely if ever been used to define new dogmas, though they frequently reaffirm doctrines that are already matters of faith. An encyclical, therefore, is an expression of the pope's ordinary teaching authority, which, according to the common teaching, is not infallible. The same may be said of apostolic exhortations, letters to priests, allocutions, homilies and the like.[30]

True to its title (and the first two Latin words of the document), *Mediator Dei* reflects a highly christological approach to the sacred liturgy. Pius XII emphasizes repeatedly that the liturgy is the work of Christ's redemption for the human race, accomplished by him as "Mediator between God and men" (n. 1).[31] With regard to the pastoral experience of the liturgy, the pope cites approvingly the work of the liturgical movement starting at the end of the nineteenth century and fostered especially by Benedictine monks in Europe. Among several recurring motifs in the encyclical are those that concern the importance of sound doctrine and teaching (e.g., nn. 8–9); the value of participation in the liturgy (e.g., n. 80); the instrumentality of ordained priests to celebrate the liturgy (e.g., n. 2); and the emphasis placed on the participation of the laity in the liturgy (e.g., n. 82). At the same time, the pope is concerned about perceived extremes fostered by some proponents of the liturgical movement, such as their criticism of the practice of private Mass (nn. 95–96); their denigration of the value of private devotions (n. 32); and their unapproved use of the vernacular (n. 59). Given that his predecessors in the papacy revived interest in the church's *lex orandi* and that its relationship to the church's *lex credendi* was a topic of great interest in the then-burgeoning liturgical movement, it is not surprising that Pius XII addressed this issue rather fully (nn. 46–48). His exposition, however, turns the expected priority to be given to *lex orandi* (n. 46) into a preference for the church's doctrine grounding its prayer: *lex credendi legem statuat supplicandi* (n. 48). With regard to the Eucharist specifically, the pope mentions "presence": "Along with the Church...her Divine Founder is present at every liturgical function: Christ is present in the august sacrifice of the altar both in the person of His minister and above all under the eucharistic species" (n. 20); the latter phrase will resurface in *Sacrosanctum Concilium*, Vatican II's Constitution on the Sacred Liturgy, (n. 7). Further on, the pope uses the term *transubstantiation* in asserting: "For by the 'transubstantiation' of bread into the body of Christ and of wine into His blood, His body and blood are both really present: now the eucharistic species under which He is present symbolize the actual separation of His body and blood" (n. 70).

But clearly the far more dominant set of terms to refer to the Eucharist is that of *sacrifice*. Following is a succinct summary of a few of the themes of the encyclical:

> Now it cannot be over-emphasized that the eucharistic sacrifice of its very nature is the unbloody immolation of the divine Victim, which is made manifest in a mystical manner by the separation of the sacred species and by their oblation to the eternal Father. Holy communion pertains to the integrity of the Mass and to the partaking of the august sacrament; but while it is obligatory for the priest who says

the Mass, it is only something earnestly recommended to the faithful. (n. 115)

In order to reiterate that each Eucharist is a sacrifice the pope asserts:

> The august sacrifice of the altar, then, is no mere empty commemoration of the passion and death of Jesus Christ, but a true and proper act of sacrifice, whereby the High Priest by an unbloody immolation offers Himself a most acceptable victim to the Eternal Father, as He did upon the cross. "It is one and the same victim; the same person now offers it by the ministry of His priests, who then offered Himself on the cross, the manner of offering alone being different." (n. 68)

The terms *immolation*, *victim*, *priests*, and *sacrifice* recall the usages at Trent.

One of the more succinct summaries of Christ's mediation as experienced in the eucharistic sacrifice is contained in number 79:

> The august sacrifice of the altar is, as it were, the supreme instrument whereby the merits won by the divine Redeemer upon the cross are distributed to the faithful: "as often as this commemorative sacrifice is offered, there is wrought the work of our Redemption." This, however, so far from lessening the dignity of the actual sacrifice on Calvary, rather proclaims and renders more manifest its greatness and its necessity, as the Council of Trent declares. Its daily immolation reminds us that there is no salvation except in the cross of our Lord Jesus Christ.

It is notable that this encyclical forthrightly asserts the involvement of the baptized:

> Moreover, the rites and prayers of the eucharistic sacrifice signify and show no less clearly that the oblation of the Victim is made by the priests in company with the people. For not only does the sacred minister, after the oblation of the bread and wine when he turns to the people, say the sig-

nificant prayer: "Pray brethren, that my sacrifice and yours may be acceptable to God the Father Almighty"; but also the prayers by which the divine Victim is offered to God are generally expressed in the plural number: and in these it is indicated more than once that the people also participate in this august sacrifice inasmuch as they offer the same. The following words, for example, are used: "For whom we offer, or who offer up to Thee....We therefore beseech thee, O Lord, to be appeased and to receive this offering of our bounded duty, as also of thy whole household....We thy servants, as also thy whole people...do offer unto thy most excellent majesty, of thine own gifts bestowed upon us, a pure victim, a holy victim, a spotless victim.[32] (n. 87)

In the previous paragraph, however, Pius XII introduces a distinction between the way the ordained priest offers the sacrifice and the way the baptized laity offer it:

This has already been stated in the clearest terms by some of Our predecessors and some Doctors of the Church. "Not only," says Innocent III of immortal memory, "do the priests offer the sacrifice, but also all the faithful: for what the priest does personally by virtue of his ministry, the faithful do collectively by virtue of their intention." We are happy to recall one of St. Robert Bellarmine's many statements on this subject. "The sacrifice," he says "is principally offered in the person of Christ. Thus the oblation that follows the consecration is a sort of attestation that the whole Church consents in the oblation made by Christ, and offers it along with Him." (n. 86)

It is at least a debated theological issue as to *how* the gathered assembly is involved in offering the eucharistic sacrifice. Among the more precise issues is how the *offerimus* language of the Roman Canon reconciles with this paragraph in *Mediator Dei*.[33]

In *Mediator Dei*, the pope uses the by-now classic terminology to describe the efficaciousness of the liturgy (nn. 27 and 36): it occurs *ex opere operato* and *ex opere operantis*, which in a second place is specified as *operantis Ecclesiae*.[34] One can only speculate whether the pope's own *Mystici Corporis* is the catalyst here. Given *Mediator Dei's* predominantly christological approach to the liturgy and the role of the ordained priest, it is notable that the pope asserts that the priest also speaks and acts "in the name of the Church."[35]

It is often claimed that Pius XII was the precursor of Vatican II through his encyclicals *Mediator Dei* on the sacred liturgy, *Mystici Corporis* on the mystical Body of Christ, and *Divino Afflante Spiritu* on the sacred scriptures. As an encyclical, *Mediator Dei* contains an exposition of the church's teaching on liturgy. Unlike the canons (or even the decrees and teaching) of Trent on the Eucharist, this document is more expressive and hortatory, even as it offers papal correctives to some conventional practices then under particular scrutiny as a result of the Liturgical Movement. At the same time it is very encouraging of many aspects of the Liturgical Movement and makes an important statement about the value of understanding and participating in the sacred liturgy. *Mediator Dei* is best read in light of *Mystici Corporis*. This combination offers an important, late-1940s reassertion of the value of seeing Eucharist and ecclesiology as intrinsically related, a theme that reemerges with full vigor with Pope John Paul II's *Ecclesia de Eucharistia* (see below).

SACROSANCTUM CONCILIUM—VATICAN II'S CONSTITUTION ON THE SACRED LITURGY (1963)

Vatican II was the second ecumenical council to have been convened since the sixteenth-century Council of Trent; the other was the First Vatican Council (1869–70). As such it deserves pride of place in terms of the relative weight we give to its Constitution on the Sacred Liturgy (1963). The Council was summoned by Pope John XXIII, who emphasized reading the "signs of the times," *aggiornamento*, and collegiality, among other things. It can be maintained that this Council was and remains a watershed event in the history of contemporary Catholicism. Even as the teachings and reforms of church life promulgated by Vatican II in general continue to be debated, it can certainly be claimed that what *Sacrosanctum Concilium* had to say about the liturgy offered nothing less than a major sea change in the way the church would approach the liturgy in general, and the Eucharist in particular, for generations to come. This is also true for the way it describes the Eucharist theologically, especially when compared with the assertions of the Council of Trent.

Clearly, the rhetoric and irenic language of this document, when compared with the decrees of Trent, are much more in line with *Mediator Dei* than with the anathemas of the canons of the Council of Trent. But it can also be said that, *like* the canons of Trent, what *Sacrosanctum Concilium* asserts about the Eucharist is (also) laconic, specific, and open-ended in the sense that what it lays forth about the reform of the liturgy was then taken up by a number of postconciliar committees that did the work of revising all of the church liturgies, something that was unprecedented in the history of the church.

The Introduction to *Sacrosanctum Concilium* (n. 2) clearly asserts that through the liturgy "the work of our redemption is accomplished."[36] This expression, which was also used in *Mediator Dei* (n. 79), has been understood as a proper starting point to develop a theology of the liturgy[37] and of the Eucharist specifically.

The Constitution on the Sacred Liturgy is divided into chapters, the first two of which are at issue here. The first is titled "General Principles for the Restoration and Promotion of the Sacred Liturgy (nn. 5–46); the second, "The Most Sacred Mystery of the Eucharist" (nn. 47–58). In the first chapter we find the important assertion that "the liturgy is the summit toward which the activity of the Church is directed; at the same time it is the font from which all her power flows" (n. 10). By way of contrast and a slight modification, the Constitution on the Church (*Lumen Gentium*) of this same Council asserts that "[t]aking part in the Eucharistic sacrifice, which is the fount and apex of the whole Christian life, they [the faithful] offer the Divine Victim to God, and offer themselves along with It" (n. 11).

That the Council's teachings in *Sacrosanctum Concilium* regarding the Eucharist are both in continuity with those of Trent and yet also break decidedly new ground is seen in many places, especially this very important paragraph on Christ's presence:

> To accomplish so great a work, Christ is always present in His Church, especially in her liturgical celebrations. He is present in the sacrifice of the Mass, not only in the person of His minister, "the same now offering, through the ministry of priests, who formerly offered himself on the cross," but especially under the Eucharistic species. By His power He is present in the sacraments, so that when a man baptizes it is really Christ Himself who baptizes. He is present in His word, since it is He Himself who speaks when the holy scriptures are read in the Church. He is present, lastly, when the Church prays and sings, for He promised: "Where two or three are gathered together in my name, there am I in the midst of them" (Matt. 18:20). (n. 7)

What is new here are the assertions about Christ's presence in the word "read in the Church" and his presence in the church herself. This paragraph has been a clarion call for appreciating the manifold presence of Christ in the celebration of the liturgy and in the Eucharist specifically.[38] Clearly, while Reformation-era polemics have come to an end, at the same time this document relies on some of Trent's decrees in its footnotes, as in, for example, "the same now offering through the ministry of priests."[39] That the Eucharist is understood to have pride of place among the sacraments is reiterated even in the first chapter (on liturgy in general), with assertions such as that "the renewal in the Eucharist of the covenant between the Lord and man draws the faithful into the compelling love of Christ and sets them on fire. From the liturgy, therefore, and especially from the Eucharist, as from a font, grace is poured forth upon us" (n. 10). This is followed by (an almost offhand?) reference to the assertion of Pius X[40] that is repeated in much subsequent magisterial literature on the liturgy, namely, that its purpose is for "the sanctification of man and the glorification of God."

The Constitution on the Sacred Liturgy clearly asserts that active participation in the liturgy is a foundational and fundamental guiding principle of the reform. For example:

> Mother Church earnestly desires that all the faithful should be led to that fully conscious, and active participation in liturgical celebrations which is demanded by the very nature of the liturgy. Such participation by the Christian people as "a chosen race, a royal priesthood, a holy nation, a redeemed people" (1 Pet. 2:9; cf. 2:4–5), is their right and duty by reason of their baptism.
>
> In the restoration and promotion of the sacred liturgy, this full and active participation by all the people is the aim to be considered before all else; for it is the primary and indispensable source from which the faithful are to derive the true Christian spirit; and therefore pastors of souls must zealously strive to achieve it, by means of the necessary instruction, in all their pastoral work. (n. 14)

That "active participation" has been emphasized not only in the design of the reforms of the liturgy but that it has been a compelling, central motif in its pastoral implementation in the United States is very clear. That its theological rationale and meaning have been so obviously at work is debated and debatable.[41] But that it remains a primary principle for the reform of the liturgy is very clear.

In chapter 2, *Sacrosanctum Concilium* addresses the Eucharist both theologically (albeit sparingly) and liturgically. The first paragraph of this chapter is rich in theological insight:

> At the Last Supper, on the night when He was betrayed, our Saviour instituted the eucharistic sacrifice of His Body and Blood. He did this in order to perpetuate the sacrifice of the Cross throughout the centuries until He should come again, and so to entrust to His beloved spouse, the Church, a memorial of His death and resurrection: a sacrament of love, a sign of unity, a bond of charity [quoting St. Augustine], a paschal banquet in which Christ is eaten, the mind is filled with grace, and a pledge of future glory is given to us [quot-

ing St. Thomas Aquinas's antiphon for Vespers, Solemnity of Corpus Christi]. (n. 47)

The integration of the terms *perpetuate, church, memorial, sacrament of love*, and *bond of charity*, along with the notions of eschatology (in two places), makes this a remarkably rich and important theological statement.

That "participation" is a goal above all others is asserted in the next paragraph, as is the assertion that the assembly offers the Immaculate Victim "not only through the Hands of the priest" but "with him":

> The Church, therefore, earnestly desires that Christ's faithful, when present at this mystery of faith, should not be there as strangers or silent spectators; on the contrary, through a good understanding of the rites and prayers they should take part in the sacred action conscious of what they are doing, with devotion and full collaboration. They should be instructed by God's word and be nourished at the table of the Lord's body; they should give thanks to God; by offering the Immaculate Victim, not only through the hands of the priest, but also with him, they should learn also to offer themselves; through Christ the Mediator, they should be drawn day by day into ever more perfect union with God and with each other, so that finally God may be all in all. (n. 48)

One of the most important assertions about the liturgical integrity of the liturgy of the Eucharist has deep theological implications:

> The two parts which, in a certain sense, go to make up the Mass, namely, the liturgy of the word and the eucharistic liturgy, are so closely connected with each other that they form but one single act of worship. Accordingly this sacred Synod strongly urges pastors of souls that, when instructing the faithful, they insistently teach them to take their part in the entire Mass, especially on Sundays and feasts of obligation. (n. 56)

This text goes a long way toward reasserting the primacy of the proclamation of the word both liturgically and theologically. It also directly challenges the understanding (presumed since before Trent) that the principal parts of the Mass are what were then called the Offertory, the Consecration, and the Priest's Communion.

How and through what processes, debates, and compromises the present *Ordo Missae* and *Missale Romanum* came to be edited and published is the topic for important current (and hopefully ongoing) research and publication.[42] That the assertions of *Sacrosanctum Concilium* created and fostered immeasurable foment and change within the Catholic Church is clear. That this foment and change occurred because of the assertions of an ecumenical council means that the changed liturgical terrain will remain with the church for generations to come.[43]

MYSTERIUM FIDEI—ENCYCLICAL OF POPE PAUL VI (1965)

Just under two years after the promulgation of *Sacrosanctum Concilium*, Pope Paul VI judged it wise to issue an encyclical to clarify the church's teaching about the Eucharist—about eucharistic presence in particular—in the face of some contemporary debates and proposed new approaches. After recommending the reforms of the liturgy mandated by *Sacrosanctum Concilium*, the pope lays out the reason for writing this encyclical:

> [S]ome of those who are dealing with this Most Holy Mystery in speech and writing are disseminating opinions on Masses celebrated in private or on the dogma of transubstantiation that are disturbing the minds of the faithful and causing them no small measure of confusion about matters of faith, just as if it were all right for someone to take doctrine that has already been defined by the Church and consign it to oblivion or else interpret it in such a way as to weaken the genuine meaning of the words or the recognized force of the concepts involved. (n. 10)[44]

The clear intent throughout most of the text is to reiterate that the eucharistic mystery involves the substantial change of bread and wine into the body and blood of the Lord. Number 11 asserts this straight-forwardly:

> [I]t is not permissible to extol the so-called "community" Mass in such a way as to detract from Masses that are cele-brated privately; or to concentrate on the notion of sacra-mental sign as if the symbolism—which no one will deny is certainly present in the Most Blessed Eucharist—fully expressed and exhausted the manner of Christ's presence in this Sacrament; or to discuss the mystery of transubstantia-tion without mentioning what the Council of Trent had to say about the marvelous conversion of the whole substance of the bread into the Body and the whole substance of the wine into the Blood of Christ, as if they involve nothing more than "transignification," or "transfinalization" as they call it; or, finally, to propose and act upon the opinion that Christ Our Lord is no longer present in the consecrated Hosts that remain after the celebration of the sacrifice of the Mass has been completed.[45]

At the same time, the encyclical also discusses the eucharistic sacrifice and who offers the sacrifice, themes that have become familiar since the Council of Trent. In addition to citing the Tridentine teaching on the Eucharist specifically, the pope also uses explicit citations from (among others) St. John Chrysostom (n. 17), St. Augustine (n. 23), St. Thomas Aquinas (n. 28), St. Bonaventure (n. 29), and St. Cyril of Jerusalem (n. 30)—as well as a whole series of texts toward the end of the document (nn. 47–51, subtitled "Writings of the Fathers") from Cyril of Jerusalem, John Chrysostom, Cyril of Alexandria, and Ambrose to bolster his argument. It is clear, however, that the teaching of Trent must be upheld even though other sources are cited and other words used to describe the Eucharist. On the one hand, the pope asserts the perennial value of the traditional language used by the church to describe the real presence (n. 23);[46] and yet on the other, he also leaves the door open to suggest that such formulations "can be made clearer and more obvious" (n. 25).[47]

The pope cites the teaching of Trent to reiterate that the Mass is the representation of the same sacrifice of Christ.[48] When addressing who offers the sacrifice, he uses the teachings of *Lumen Gentium* from Vatican II as a main support for his argument:

> But there is something else that We would like to add that is very helpful in shedding light on the mystery of the Church; We mean the fact that the whole Church plays the role of priest and victim along with Christ, offering the Sacrifice of the Mass and itself completely offered in it. The Fathers of the Church taught this wondrous doctrine [citing St. Augustine]. A few years ago Our predecessor of happy memory, Pius XII, explained it [citing *Mediator Dei*] and only recently the Second Vatican Council reiterated it in its Constitution on the Church, in dealing with the people of God [citing *Lumen Gentium*, n. 11]. To be sure, the distinction between the universal priesthood and the hierarchical priesthood is something essential and not just a matter of degree, and it has to be maintained in a proper way [ibid., n. 10]. Yet We cannot help being filled with an earnest desire to see this teaching explained over and over until it takes deep root in the hearts of the faithful. For it is a most effective means of fostering devotion to the Eucharist, of extolling the dignity of all the faithful, and of spurring them on to reach the heights of sanctity, which means the total and generous offering of oneself to the service of the Divine Majesty. (n. 31)

"Immolation" language recurs when the pope asserts:

> The few things that We have touched upon concerning the Sacrifice of the Mass encourage Us to say something about the Sacrament of the Eucharist, since both Sacrifice and Sacrament pertain to the same mystery and cannot be separated from each other. The Lord is immolated in an unbloody way in the Sacrifice of the Mass and He re-presents the sacrifice of the Cross and applies its salvific power at the moment

when he becomes sacramentally present—through the words of consecration—as the spiritual food of the faithful, under the appearances of bread and wine. (n. 34)

The next two paragraphs are often cited because they amplify what was asserted in *Sacrosanctum Concilium* about Christ being present in works of mercy and the proclamation of the word:

> 35. All of us realize that there is more than one way in which Christ is present in His Church. We want to go into this very joyful subject, which the Constitution on the Sacred Liturgy presented briefly, at somewhat greater length. Christ is present in His Church when she prays, since He is the one who "prays for us and prays in us and to whom we pray: He prays for us as our priest, He prays in us as our head, He is prayed to by us as our God" [citing St. Augustine, *On the Psalms*]; and He is the one who has promised, "Where two or three are gathered together in my name, I am there in the midst of them" [Mt. 18:20]. He is present in the Church as she performs her works of mercy, not just because whatever good we do to one of His least brethren we do to Christ Himself [Mt. 25:40], but also because Christ is the one who performs these works through the Church and who continually helps men with His divine love. He is present in the Church as she moves along on her pilgrimage with a longing to reach the portals of eternal life, for He is the one who dwells in our hearts through faith, and who instills charity in them through the Holy Spirit whom He gives to us.

> 36. In still another very genuine way, He is present in the Church as she preaches, since the Gospel which she proclaims is the word of God, and it is only in the name of Christ, the Incarnate Word of God, and by His authority and with His help that it is preached, so that there might be "one flock resting secure in one shepherd."

Again, what is very significant here is the assertion that Christ is present in the performing of works of mercy and in preaching. The latter reference is fully in line with this pope's concern for evangelization, specifically in his later encyclical *Evangelium Nuntiandi*. That this is also a recurring and important theme in the theology of Pope Benedict XVI will be seen below.

Not surprisingly, Paul VI then emphasizes the "real" presence:

> 38. These various ways in which Christ is present fill the mind with astonishment and offer the Church a mystery for her contemplation. But there is another way in which Christ is present in His Church, a way that surpasses all the others. It is His presence in the Sacrament of the Eucharist, which is, for this reason, "a more consoling source of devotion, a lovelier object of contemplation and holier in what it contains" than all the other sacraments; for it contains Christ Himself and it is "a kind of consummation of the spiritual life, and in a sense the goal of all the sacraments" [citing St. Thomas Aquinas].

> 39. This presence is called "real" not to exclude the idea that the others are "real" too, but rather to indicate presence par excellence, because it is substantial and through it Christ becomes present whole and entire, God and man [citing Trent]. And so it would be wrong for anyone to try to explain this manner of presence by dreaming up a so-called "pneumatic" nature of the glorious body of Christ that would be present everywhere; or for anyone to limit it to symbolism, as if this most sacred Sacrament were to consist in nothing more than an efficacious sign "of the spiritual presence of Christ and of His intimate union with the faithful, the members of His Mystical Body" [citing Pius XII's *Humani Generis*].

The pope then directly challenges any contemporary emphasis on "symbolism" (nn. 40–46) and reiterates the teaching of Trent that Christ is present through a "truly wonderful conversion that the Catholic Church fittingly and properly calls transubstantiation" (n. 46). With regard to appropriate practices, the pope repeatedly calls for the daily celebration of Mass (even privately) and for eucharistic adoration (nn. 64–69).

Mysterium Fidei had a targeted focus, namely, to reiterate the Catholic Church's traditional teaching on the permanent reality of the real presence of Christ in the Eucharist. Yet its openness to possible other formulations and the teaching that "presence" includes works of mercy and the proclamation of the word need to be kept in mind as we survey even more recent documents on the Eucharist.

CATECHISM OF THE CATHOLIC CHURCH (1992)

In his apostolic constitution *Fidei Depositum* introducing the *Catechism*, Pope John Paul II addressed its doctrinal value. He stated that the *Catechism* "is a statement of the Church's faith and of catholic doctrine, attested to or illuminated by Sacred Scripture, the Apostolic Tradition, and the Church's Magisterium. I declare it to be a sure norm for teaching the faith and thus a valid and legitimate instrument for ecclesial communion."[49] In addressing the authority of the *Catechism*, Francis Sullivan invokes Joseph Ratzinger when he states that "the individual doctrines that the *Catechism* affirms have no other authority than that which they already possess."[50] Therefore, we should look to the *Catechism* not for anything new, but for a distillation of teaching in an orderly way. Compared with the (American) *Baltimore Catechisms* that were in use catechetically up to Vatican II, the 1992 *Catechism* is expository and ample in style.[51] The *Baltimore Catechisms* were apologetic, in a question-and-answer format. (It is noteworthy that the statement in *Anglicanorum Coetibus* that the norm for understanding Catholic doctrine is *The Catechism of the Catholic Church* was in response to the request of the petitioners that was acceded to by The Holy See; it was not initiated by the Holy See itself.)[52]

The sacraments are discussed in part 2 of the *Catechism*, "The Celebration of the Christian Mystery." Section 1 is "The Sacramental Economy," and it is important for the way in which it contextualizes the subsequent material on the liturgy and sacraments, specifically the liturgy as the work of the Trinity, the paschal mystery in the sacraments, and the sacramental celebration of the paschal mystery.[53] This is followed in turn by section 2, "The Seven Sacraments of the Church." In this section, chapters 1 and 2 are about the sacraments of Christian initiation, namely, baptism and confirmation.[54]

In its specific treatment of the Eucharist, the *Catechism* refers to it as the completion of Christian initiation (n. 1322) and as the "source and summit of ecclesial life" (n. 1324). In a deceptively short single page (nn. 1329–32), the *Catechism* notes the following "names" for the Eucharist and offers a comment on each: "action of thanksgiving"; "the breaking of bread"; "eucharistic assembly"; "memorial"; "holy sacrifice" (under which it names "holy sacrifice of the Mass," "sacrifice of praise," "spiritual sacrifice," and "pure and holy sacrifice"); "holy and divine liturgy" (under which it cites "sacred mysteries" and "most blessed sacrament"); "holy communion" (under which it names "holy things" [*ta hagia; sancta*], "bread of angels," "bread from heaven," "medicine of immortality," and "viaticum"); and finally the "Holy Mass" (*Missa*). This list is followed in turn by a longer consideration of the Eucharist in the economy of salvation, including the signs of bread and wine, the institution of the Eucharist, and the command to "do this in memory of me" (nn. 1333–44). This kaleidoscope of images mirrors nothing less than a mosaic of possible images for describing the Eucharist that should always be taken together and seen in relationship with one another.[55]

The *Catechism* next provides a treatment of the Mass of all ages, the very expansive description of the movement of celebration with its various parts, and a fulsome consideration of the parts of the Eucharistic Prayers and their particular meanings (nn. 1345–55). Numbers 1352 to 55 reflect a more specifically liturgical theology of the Eucharist. From there, the *Catechism* moves to "the sacramental sacrifice" and "the presence of Christ" (nn. 1356–81). That these are so rich in ecclesiology and contain a number of scriptural and liturgical references and texts from theologians such as St. Thomas Aquinas is very significant, especially when compared with some of the earlier documents cited above, such as those from Trent. The final material on the Eucharist concerns the paschal banquet, and is useful again for both its rich ecclesiology, as well as its comparatively brief conclusion about eschatology (nn. 1382–1401).

ECCLESIA DE EUCHARISTIA—
ENCYCLICAL OF POPE JOHN PAUL II (2003)

Beginning with *Dominicae Cenae* in 1980, Pope John Paul II wrote an annual letter to priests on various aspects of the Eucharist and of priestly ordination. He chose to broaden this practice in 2003 to write the encyclical letter *Ecclesia de Eucharistia* (*EE*) to the whole church, expanding on the themes from *Dominicae Cenae* (n. 9).[56] He explicitly refers in the body of the text to the teachings of Trent, *Mediator Dei*, *Mysterium Fidei*, and the Vatican II Constitutions *Lumen Gentium* and *Sacrosanctum Concilium* (n. 9). He then goes on to assert that there have been many positive elements in the reform of the liturgy since Vatican II:

> The Magisterium's commitment to proclaiming the Eucharistic mystery has been matched by interior growth within the Christian community. Certainly *the liturgical reform inaugurated by the Council* has greatly contributed to a more conscious, active and fruitful participation in the Holy Sacrifice of the Altar on the part of the faithful. In many places, *adoration of the Blessed Sacrament* is also an important daily practice and becomes an inexhaustible source of holiness. The devout participation of the faithful in the Eucharistic procession on the Solemnity of the Body and Blood of Christ is a grace from the Lord which yearly brings joy to those who take part in it.
>
> Other positive signs of eucharistic faith and love might also be mentioned. (*EE*, n. 10)[57]

He then proceeds to offer some observations that, in his judgment, need to be addressed in this encyclical:

> Unfortunately, alongside these lights, *there are also shadows*. In some places the practice of Eucharistic adoration has been almost completely abandoned. In various parts of the Church abuses have occurred, leading to confusion with regard to sound faith and Catholic doctrine concerning this wonderful sacrament. At times one encounters an extremely

reductive understanding of the Eucharistic mystery. Stripped of its sacrificial meaning, it is celebrated as if it were simply a fraternal banquet. Furthermore, the necessity of the ministerial priesthood, grounded in apostolic succession, is at times obscured and the sacramental nature of the Eucharist is reduced to its mere effectiveness as a form of proclamation. This has led here and there to ecumenical initiatives which, albeit well-intentioned, indulge in Eucharistic practices contrary to the discipline by which the Church expresses her faith. How can we not express profound grief at all this? The Eucharist is too great a gift to tolerate ambiguity and depreciation.

It is my hope that the present Encyclical Letter will effectively help to banish the dark clouds of unacceptable doctrine and practice, so that the Eucharist will continue to shine forth in all its radiant mystery. (*EE*, n. 10)

On balance, the document is rich in its theology of Eucharist and is especially notable because of its eucharistic ecclesiology. By considering the Eucharist within its (native) ecclesiological context, the pope returns to the way the magisterium of the first millennium treated the Eucharist in relation to questions and practices in the church at large.[58] Like other encyclicals, this is captured in the opening statement that "the Church draws her life from the Eucharist" (n. 1). The titles of the key chapters bear this out: "The Eucharist Builds the Church" (chapter 2); "The Apostolicity of the Eucharist and of the Church" (chapter 3); and "The Eucharist and Ecclesial Communion" (chapter 4).

Because of its breadth and because the pope explicitly refers to and uses previous church teaching on the Eucharist, it is appropriate to delineate what is new or of particular import in this letter as compared with what has preceded it. For example, its tone is far more irenic than that of the teachings of Trent, some assertions of Pius XII's in *Mediator Dei*, and some of Paul VI's in *Mysterium Fidei*.

Throughout his encyclical, John Paul II uses texts and rites of the revised liturgy to illustrate a point he is making about, for example, the paschal mystery, the paschal Triduum, and the Eucharistic mystery (n. 2).[59] He illustrates one of his assertions about the sacrificial nature of the Eucharist by using the text of the Institution Narrative, which states explicitly that the body and blood are "given for you."[60] He asserts that there is a "cosmic character" to the Eucharist (n. 8). It is always "in some way celebrated *on the altar of the world. It unites heaven and earth. It embraces and permeates all creation. The Son of God became man in order to restore all creation, in one supreme act of praise, to the One who made it from nothing.*"

The pope helpfully combines two texts from Vatican II in referring to the way the whole church offers the Eucharist: "Taking part in the Eucharistic Sacrifice, which is the source and summit of the whole Christian life, they offer the divine victim to God, and offer themselves along with it" (*EE*, n. 13; drawing from *Lumen Gentium*, n. 11, and *Sacrosanctum Concilium*, n. 48). It is notable that when he addresses the relationship between the celebration of the Eucharist and daily life the pontiff speaks of the tension between the "here and now" experience of Christ in this life through the Eucharist and our longed-for union with him at the end of time—"thy kingdom come." This is typical of the pope's concern to see things as a theological whole. It is not Eucharist *and* good deeds but Eucharist *as helping us* to see that "we are not there yet" ("thy kingdom come") and to see that in the meantime what we "have" in this life is really not our possession. Rather, we are stewards of all that has been given to us and, therefore, what we have is ours to share.[61] In the entire Christian life and as celebrated in the Eucharist, there is always an eschatological tension between the "already" and the "not yet" which requires that in the meantime we share what we have with those who have not—that we address the immediate concerns of our neighbors even as we await the fulfillment of the Eucharist and all of the Christian life in the kingdom of God forever.

It is unclear why the pope adapts the classic patristic adage in his statement that "the Eucharist builds [as opposed to "makes"] the Church and the Church makes the Eucharist, it follows that there is a profound relationship between the two" (n. 20), but he uses it never-theless to underscore his main ecclesiological message. He reiterates his basic approach to sacred ordination established in *Dominicae Cenae*, that the priest acts *in persona Christi*. He cites *Lumen Gentium*, n. 10, when he states that the priest "brings about the Eucharistic Sacrifice and offers it to God in the name of all the people" (*EE*, n. 28). He then continues:

> [I]n persona Christi means more than offering "in the name of" or "in the place of" Christ. *In persona* means in specific sacramental identification with the eternal High Priest who is author and principal subject of this sacrifice of his, a sacrifice in which, in truth, nobody can take his place....This minister is a gift which the assembly *receives through episcopal succession going back to the Apostles*. It is the Bishop who, through the Sacrament of Holy Orders, makes a new presbyter [note the term *presbyter* as opposed to *sacerdos*[62]] by conferring upon him the power to consecrate the Eucharist. Consequently, the Eucharistic mystery cannot be celebrated in any community except by an ordained priest, as the Fourth Lateran Council expressly taught. (*EE*, n. 29)[63]

That the documents of Vatican II assiduously avoid the term *alter Christus* is important to note, as is the fact that *in persona Christi* is often followed by the phrase *capitis ecclesiae*. There is a helpful body of literature assessing just what *in persona Christi* does and does not mean.[64]

The issue of intercommunion, not yet found in the documents treated thus far, is introduced at this point in *Ecclesia de Eucharistia* (and returns to it in numbers 45 and 46):

> 30. The Catholic faithful, therefore, while respecting the religious convictions of those separated brethren, must refrain from receiving the communion distributed in their celebrations, so as not to condone an ambiguity about the nature of the Eucharist and, consequently, to fail in their duty to bear clear witness to the truth....

> 32. [T]his requires the presence of a presbyter [again note the term *presbyter*, not *priest*], who alone is qualified to offer the Eucharist *in persona Christi*. When a community lacks a priest, attempts are rightly made somehow to remedy the situation so that it can continue its Sunday celebrations.

When addressing the "ecclesiology of communion," the pope asserts that "the Eucharist thus appears as the culmination of all the sacraments in perfecting our communion with God the Father by identification with his only-begotten Son through the working of the Holy Spirit" (n. 34) but that "the celebration of the Eucharist, however, cannot be the starting-point for communion; it presupposes that communion already exists" (n. 35). Quoting St. John Chrysostom, he implores that "no one draw near to this sacred table with a sullied and corrupt conscience" (n. 36), and that "*the Lord's Day* also becomes *the Day of the Church*, when she can effectively exercise her role as the sacrament of unity" (n. 41).[65]

Because of the importance the pope places on the ecclesiology of the Eucharist, it is important to cite at length from what he says in chapter 4, "The Eucharist and Ecclesial Communion":

> 44. Precisely because the Church's unity, which the Eucharist brings about through the Lord's sacrifice and by communion in his body and blood, absolutely requires full communion in the bonds of the profession of faith, the sacraments and ecclesiastical governance, it is not possible to celebrate together the same Eucharistic liturgy until those bonds are fully re-established. Any such concelebration would not be a valid means, and might well prove instead to be *an obstacle, to the attainment of full communion*, by weakening the sense of how far we remain from this goal and by introducing or exacerbating ambiguities with regard to one or another truth of the faith. The path towards full unity can only be undertaken in truth. In this area, the prohibitions of Church law leave no room for uncertainty, in fidelity to the moral norm laid down by the Second Vatican Council.
>
> I would like nonetheless to reaffirm what I said in my Encyclical Letter *Ut Unum Sint* after having acknowledged the impossibility of Eucharistic sharing: "And yet we do have a burning desire to join in celebrating the one Eucharist of the Lord, and this desire itself is already a common prayer of

praise, a single supplication. Together we speak to the Father and increasingly we do so 'with one heart'".

45. While it is never legitimate to concelebrate in the absence of full communion, the same is not true with respect to the administration of the Eucharist *under special circumstances, to individual persons* belonging to Churches or Ecclesial Communities not in full communion with the Catholic Church. In this case, in fact, the intention is to meet a grave spiritual need for the eternal salvation of an individual believer, not to bring about an *intercommunion* which remains impossible until the visible bonds of ecclesial communion are fully re-established.

This was the approach taken by the Second Vatican Council when it gave guidelines for responding to Eastern Christians separated in good faith from the Catholic Church, who spontaneously ask to receive the Eucharist from a Catholic minister and are properly disposed. This approach was then ratified by both Codes, which also consider—with necessary modifications—the case of other non-Eastern Christians who are not in full communion with the Catholic Church.

46. In my Encyclical *Ut Unum Sint* I expressed my own appreciation of these norms, which make it possible to provide for the salvation of souls with proper discernment: "It is a source of joy to note that Catholic ministers are able, in certain particular cases, to administer the sacraments of the Eucharist, Penance and Anointing of the Sick to Christians who are not in full communion with the Catholic Church but who greatly desire to receive these sacraments, freely request them and manifest the faith which the Catholic Church professes with regard to these sacraments. Conversely, in specific cases and in particular circumstances, Catholics too can request these same sacraments from ministers of Churches in which these sacraments are valid.

These conditions, from which no dispensation can be given, must be carefully respected, even though they deal with specific individual cases, because the denial of one or more truths of the faith regarding these sacraments and, among these, the truth regarding the need of the ministerial priesthood for their validity, renders the person asking improperly disposed to legitimately receiving them. And the opposite is also true: Catholics may not receive communion in those communities which lack a valid sacrament of Orders.

When the pope first introduced the issue of intercommunion in this encyclical (in numbers 30 and 32, as mentioned above), he immediately addressed a number of related issues, including "the sacramental incompleteness" (n. 32) of Sunday celebrations in the absence of a priest, or of services of the word only, even though there might also be provision for the distribution of holy communion.[66] That this has been reiterated in church documents comparatively frequently since *Ecclesia de Eucharistia* would seem to indicate real concern that the enactment of the whole reality of the Eucharist within Mass is not being perceived as a requirement central to the Catholic faith.

Two additional themes occupy the last part of the encyclical: the creativity of artists supporting the dignity of Eucharistic celebration (chapter 5) and Mary under the title of Woman of the Eucharist (chapter 6).

Toward the end of chapter 5, the pope asserts the following about the dignity of the celebration: "I have asked the competent offices of the Roman Curia to prepare a more specific document, including prescriptions of a juridical nature, on this very important subject. No one is permitted to undervalue the mystery entrusted to our hands: it is too great for anyone to feel free to treat lightly and with disregard for its sacredness and its universality" (n. 52). This directive resulted in the publication, the following year, of *Redemptionis Sacramentum*.

Noticeably absent in this encyclical, especially given the topic's prominence in Paul VI's *Mysterium Fidei*, is any reference to the proclamation of the word of God and to preaching at Mass. That there is much richness here theologically, especially regarding ecclesiology, communion, and apostolicity, is clear. Despite the fact that he did not live to preside over it, it was Pope John Paul II who convoked the 2005

Synod, The Eucharist: Source and Summit of the Life and Mission of the Church. One could legitimately argue that Pope Benedict XVI's request that the 2008 Synod, The Word of God in the Life and Mission of the Church, should be seen as a parallel and supplement to the 2005 Synod on the Eucharist, just as his postsynodal exhortation *Sacramentum Caritatis* is (discussed below). Here the parallel taught in *Sacrosanctum Concilium* ("that the liturgy of the word and the Eucharistic liturgy form one act of worship" [n. 56]) can be seen as in the combination of these two synods together.

In the end, the encyclical *Ecclesia de Eucharistia* in the tradition of important church documents and ecclesiastical authors (especially in the patristic era) that addressed the important (and always presumed) relationship of the Eucharist to the church.

REDEMPTIONIS SACRAMENTUM—INSTRUCTION FROM THE CONGREGATION FOR DIVINE WORSHIP AND THE DISCIPLINE OF THE SACRAMENTS (2004)

Most of the post–Vatican II liturgical rites were promulgated by a decree from the Congregation for Divine Worship and the Discipline of the Sacraments with a mandate of the pope.[67] The same is asserted in the concluding paragraph of *Redemptionis Sacramentum*, which states that "this Instruction [note the term] [was] prepared by the Congregation for Divine Worship and the Discipline of the Sacraments by the mandate of the Supreme Pontiff John Paul II...[who] ordered it to be published and to be observed immediately by all concerned."[68] The often-used distinction between a "juridical" document and a "theological" one is blurred here simply because there are copious references to the church's teaching on the Eucharist and its liturgical practice. At the same time it is clear that the burden of this document is to direct the proper celebration of the Mass and to correct abuses. It is less about the church's beliefs about the Eucharist than about the way the church celebrates the Eucharist.

By design, the Instruction first deals with the regulation of the sacred liturgy (nn. 14–34) and participation in the liturgy (nn. 36–47). It then gives specific directives (and corrections) on the proper celebration of Mass, communion, Eucharistic reservation, and "extraordinary functions of the lay faithful" (nn. 146–53). The role of the ordained priest is emphasized throughout, which is in line with Pope John Paul II's teachings given throughout his pontificate.

That the document notes the importance of *lex orandi, lex credendi* (n. 10) is useful, especially since it takes no position on Pius XII's framing of that discussion, that is, the priority of the *lex credendi* in shaping liturgical prayers. By far the most dominant perspective for understanding the Eucharist is that of sacrifice (nn. 38, 42, 48, 50, 110, 129, 134, 140, and 172). The Eucharist as a sacrament is noted in number 48; also noted is that it is an antidote to preserve us from sins (n. 80).

A chapter dealing with remedies to be applied to liturgical abuses represents a new addition to postconciliar documents about the Eucharist (nn. 169–84). Further on, the Instruction delineates *graviora delicta* (about abuses to the Eucharistic species) and "grave matters" that put at risk the validity and dignity of the Mass.[69] Toward the end of the Instruction we find the statement that any Catholic "has the right to lodge a complaint regarding a liturgical abuse to the diocesan Bishop or to the competent Ordinary…or to the Apostolic See" (n. 184). This is an unprecedented assertion in official post–Vatican II liturgical documents.

Although it could be said that this document does not concern the theology of the Eucharist, nevertheless, the fact that it takes very seriously the way the Mass is celebrated and the way the Eucharist is treated is important, since eucharistic practice always reflects belief and vice versa.[70] One example in this instruction concerns liturgical roles. A notable and positive contribution of the postconciliar liturgical reform has been the restoration of the variety of roles to a number of ordained and nonordained persons. While the tone of the admonitions and corrections in *Redemptionis Sacramentum* can be judged to be harsh, at the same time there is a theology of liturgical roles behind such judgments; these include, among others, comments about the danger of "clericalization" (n. 45) and about male altar servers (n. 47), an admonition that only priests are to recite the Eucharistic Prayer (n. 52), a reminder to priests not to break the host at the words "he broke the bread" during the Eucharistic Prayer (n. 55), and the requirement that only the sacred scriptures be read at the liturgy (n. 62).

MANE NOBISCUM DOMINE—APOSTOLIC LETTER OF POPE JOHN PAUL II FOR THE "YEAR OF THE EUCHARIST" (OCTOBER 2004–OCTOBER 2005)

Mane Nobiscum Domine ("Stay with us, Lord")[71] is an exhortation to the church to focus on the Eucharist in the year leading to the Synod on the Eucharist. As is typical of such letters, it draws on several of the pope's prior teachings, including *Tertio Millennio Adveniente* (On the Coming of the New Millennium [1994]), *Redemptor Hominis* (1979), and *Dies Domini, Ecclesia de Eucharistia*, and *Rosarium Virginis Mariae* (all 2002). This letter is brief and bears none of the more neuralgic items or negative tone contained in *Redemptionis Sacramentum*.

Mane Nobiscum Domine continually reiterates that the faithful are to lead a eucharistic life and emphasizes that *"the Eucharist is a mystery of light!"* (n. 11). Part of the light shed by the Eucharist comes from the proclamation of the word of God. The pope asserts that the Mass is composed of "two tables," that of the word and that of the bread (n. 12). The "table of the word" contains a treasury of the proclaimed scriptures (n. 13). While no single aspect of the eucharistic mystery can capture its fullness, nevertheless the pope notes its sacrificial nature (n. 15), that it is the *"mystery of the 'real' presence"* (n. 16), and that *"Eucharistic adoration outside Mass"* is therefore to be encouraged (n. 18).

The pope returns to a major theme from *Ecclesia de Eucharistia* in speaking about how the Eucharist is "the source and manifestation of communion" (chapter 3, especially numbers 21 to 22). Some particular features in chapter 4 on relating the Eucharist and mission have not been seen in the other documents under consideration here. For example, the pope speaks about the consequence of celebrating the Eucharist and the project of the church's mission in the world as a result of its eucharistic celebration. The Eucharist is a *"project of solidarity* for all of humanity" and should spur us to *"communion, peace and solidarity"* (n. 27). Again, these examples concern what some contemporary liturgical theologians call the *lex agendi* or the *lex vivendi*[72] of the Eucharist.

SACRAMENTUM CARITATIS— POSTSYNODAL EXHORTATION OF POPE BENEDICT XVI (2007)

In assessing the value of the final reports issued after the meetings of the synod and in its (now customary) postsynodal exhortations written by the Holy Father, Avery Dulles observes:

> The reports issuing from assemblies of the Synod deserve to be received with respect, especially because they have been approved by the pope before being promulgated. Frequently the pope summarizes the results of these assemblies by writing Post-Synodal Apostolic Exhortations that enjoy his personal authority. The exact ecclesial status of the Synod of Bishops is still in flux and is debated among experts.[73]

An extended period is allowed prior to synods to debate and discuss the topic at hand; this pre-synod discussion is fostered by the publication (typically) of two documents, first the *lineamenta* and then the *instrumentum laboris*.[74] Because they reflect the debates held on the synod floor, the "final propositions" are worth particular consideration, especially in this case[75] since many were eventually incorporated into *Sacramentum Caritatis*.[76]

Even though it is not an encyclical, the first two words of *Sacramentum Caritatis* recall the first words (and title) of Pope Benedict's *Deus Caritas Est*. The exhortation's considerations on the Eucharist are divided into three parts, titled—

"A Mystery to Be Believed"
"A Mystery to Be Celebrated"
"A Mystery to Be Lived"

The main emphasis throughout the exhortation is on the celebration of the Eucharist, even though adoration and devotion are also noted (nn. 6 and 69). This document differs markedly from the rest of those under review here, not only in structure but also in content. It is intended to be an overview of the church's belief, practice, and mission as related to the Eucharist.

The decidedly trinitarian emphasis in part 1—"A Mystery to Be Believed"—and its particular reference to the Holy Spirit (nn. 7–8, 12–13) are particularly welcome. Appropriately, the balance of this section deals with the relationship of the Eucharist to the church (nn. 14–15), to the other sacraments (n. 16–32), and to eschatology (nn. 30–32). The Virgin Mary is mentioned in number 32.

In part 2—"A Mystery to Be Celebrated"—Benedict XVI expounds on his reference to the importance the synod placed on "the connection between the *lex orandi* and *lex credendi*" (n. 34), and he makes extensive use of the church's *orandi* (both texts and rites). Here he highlights the eucharistic *actio* in which the whole church takes part—*Christus totus in capite et in corpore* (citing St. Augustine extensively). The Liturgy of the Word receives due emphasis here (nn. 44–46), and he cites the phrase "two tables" to show the equality of and intrinsic connection between the Liturgy of the Word and the eucharistic liturgy. The prominence given here to the importance of the homily can be related to the pope's later encouragement about a contemporary "mystagogical catechesis" (n. 64).

Just as he earlier referred to the cosmos when discussing the institution of the Eucharist (n. 10), so here, too, in the section on the presentation of the gifts, the pope notes the relationship between the cosmos and the eucharistic action (n. 47). That "active participation" occupies a central place in this part is significant (nn. 53–63); it also includes a reference to Christians who are not Catholic (n. 56).

Part 3 of the exhortation is titled "A Mystery to Be Lived." Perhaps most important—simply because it has not received this kind of attention in the other texts under discussion here, and also because of its significance in the Christian life—is that the entire third part concerns the relationship between the Eucharist and Christian life (nn. 70–93). Among the subtopics worth noting in this section are the observance of the Lord's Day (nn. 72–74); Sunday celebrations in the absence of a priest (at which communion need not be distributed; n. 75); the relation of the Eucharist to culture (n. 77–78); the lay faithful (n. 79); priestly spirituality (n. 80); and the consecrated life. Certainly among the most topical assertions in the document concerns "eucharistic consistency" and the relation of the Eucharist to belief and daily life:

> Here it is important to consider what the Synod Fathers described as *eucharistic consistency*, a quality which our lives are objectively called to embody. Worship pleasing to God can never be a purely private matter, without consequences for our relationships with others: it demands a public witness to our faith. Evidently, this is true for all the baptized, yet it is especially incumbent upon those who, by virtue of their social or political position, must make decisions regarding fundamental values, such as respect for human life, its defense from conception to natural death, the family built upon marriage between a man and a woman, the freedom to educate one's children and the promotion of the common good in all its forms. These values are not negotiable. Consequently, Catholic politicians and legislators, conscious of their grave responsibility before society, must feel particularly bound, on the basis of a properly formed conscience, to introduce and support laws inspired by values grounded in human nature. There is an objective connection here with the Eucharist (cf. *1 Cor* 11:27–29). Bishops are bound to reaffirm constantly these values as part of their responsibility to the flock entrusted to them. (n. 83)

The importance of mission and witness is also noted very thoroughly and carefully (nn. 84–85).[77]

This emphasis is focused and deepened in what follows: the social implications of the eucharistic mystery (n. 89), the church's social teaching (n. 91), and the sanctification of life and the protection of creation (n. 92). These are all new to church documents on the Eucharist. In treating of "the sanctification of the world and the protection of creation," the pope writes:

> Finally, to develop a profound eucharistic spirituality that is also capable of significantly affecting the fabric of society, the Christian people, in giving thanks to God through the Eucharist, should be conscious that they do so in the name of all creation, aspiring to the sanctification of the world and working intensely to that end. The Eucharist itself powerfully illuminates human history and the whole cosmos. In this sacramental perspective we learn, day by day, that every ecclesial event is a kind of sign by which God makes himself known and challenges us. The eucharistic form of life can thus help foster a real change in the way we approach history and the world. The liturgy itself teaches us this, when, during the presentation of the gifts, the priest raises to God a prayer of blessing and petition over the bread and wine, "fruit of the earth," "fruit of the vine" and "work of human hands." (n. 92)[78]

In this document the pope refers to two possible adjustments in the Order of Mass. The first concerns the location of the Sign of Peace (n. 49, fn. 150) as was discussed during the synod. Subsequently the Congregation for Divine Worship consulted with episcopal conferences about relocating it from its present position before communion.[79] No decision has been made. The second possible adjustment concerns the words of dismissal at the end of Mass:

The dismissal: "Ite, missa est"

> 51. Finally, I would like to comment briefly on the observations of the Synod Fathers regarding the dismissal at the end of the eucharistic celebration. After the blessing, the deacon or the priest dismisses the people with the words: *Ite, missa est.* These words help us to grasp the relationship between the Mass just celebrated and the mission of

Christians in the world. In antiquity, *missa* simply meant "dismissal." However in Christian usage it gradually took on a deeper meaning. The word "dismissal" has come to imply a "mission." These few words succinctly express the missionary nature of the Church. The People of God might be helped to understand more clearly this essential dimension of the Church's life, taking the dismissal as a starting point. In this context, it might also be helpful to provide new texts, duly approved, for the prayer over the people and the final blessing, in order to make this connection clear.

In addition to *Ite, missa est*, whose present translation is "the Mass is ended, go in peace," there are three other new dismissals: "*Ite ad Evangelium Domini annuntiandum*" ("Go and announce the Gospel of the Lord"); "*Ite in pace, glorificando vita vestra Dominum*" ("Go in peace, glorifying the Lord by your life"); and "*Ite in pace*" ("Go in peace").

As a document, *Sacramentaum Caritatis* stands alongside other postsynodal exhortations in terms of style and scope.[80] In its description of the eucharistic mystery, it stands alongside the contents and style of the *Catechism of the Catholic Church* (nn. 1322–1419). Its use of the church's *lex orandi, lex credendi* serves as an example of an ecclesiastical document that should be emulated in developing a eucharistic theology always in relation to the church's rites. In its emphasis on mission and witness, it is a model of Eucharistic spirituality. That it devotes a section to preserving creation as part of the consequences of celebrating the Eucharist reflects (perhaps tangentially) Pope John Paul II's use of the phrase "altar of the world" in *Ecclesia de Eucharistia*. It is an important reminder that the sacramental system is based on the presumed use of creation and the use of manufactured bread and wine for the Eucharist.

SUMMORUM PONTIFICUM—APOSTOLIC LETTER OF POPE BENEDICT XVI (2007)

The Roman Missal promulgated after the Council of Trent (1570), and as used during the pontificate of Blessed John XXIII

(1962), was regarded after the Council as the "extraordinary form" of the Roman Rite. On July 7, 2007, Pope Benedict XVI published the apostolic letter *Summorum Pontificum* on the use of preconciliar liturgical forms, specifically, the Mass as promulgated after the Council of Trent.[81] The letter was a *motu proprio*—a document that is written by the pope on his own initiative, that is addressed to the entire church, and that can be either administrative or doctrinal in nature.

The *motu proprio* was accompanied by a "letter" from the Holy Father addressed to his brother bishops regarding "news reports and judgments made without sufficient information" that, he said, had "created no little confusion."[82] The *motu proprio* had been long anticipated: the proposal for the possibility of increased use of the Mass as reformed after Trent had been discussed at the Synod on the Eucharist held in Rome in October 2005; it was also one of the topics discussed by the heads of Roman curial offices in December 2005 and at a meeting of the College of Cardinals on March 24, 2006. On each of these occasions, the idea for expanding the existing permission to use this form of the Missal received little traction.[83] Behind this expanded permission, however, is the issue of reconciliation within Catholicism of the followers of Archbishop Lefebvre who are devoted to the continued use of the Missal as revised after Trent.[84] No pope wants to die with a schism on his watch, and Pope John Paul II was no different. Hence, from early on in his pontificate he took steps to assess the depth and rationale for the separation of the Lefebvre followers from the rest of the Catholic communion and sought their reconciliation. Pope Benedict XVI followed in this line with his *motu proprio*.

One can trace three stages to the evolution toward *Summorum Pontificum*:[85]

Stage 1: On October 3, 1984, the Congregation for Divine Worship issued a circular letter entitled *Quattuor Abhinc Annos*. The context for it was those who had remained attached to the so-called Tridentine Mass (as distinguished from the Tridentine Rite) either because of age or because they were followers of Archbishop Lefebvre. It stated:

The diocesan bishop may allow those who are explicitly named in a petition submitted to him to celebrate Mass by use of the 1962 *editio typica* of the Roman Missal.

There must be unequivocal, even public evidence that the priest and people petitioning have no ties with those who impugn the lawfulness and doctrinal soundness of the Roman Missal promulgated in 1970 by Pope Paul VI.

This indult is to be used without prejudice to the liturgical reform that is to be observed in the life of each ecclesial community.[86]

Stage 2: In 1988, there occurred what the Vatican had wanted to stave off, namely, the ordination of four bishops as followers of Archbishop Lefebvre. They were summarily excommunicated. On July 2 of that same year Pope John Paul II himself issued the apostolic letter *Ecclesia Dei* in which he stated:

> To all those Catholic faithful who feel attached to some previous liturgical and disciplinary forms of the Latin tradition I wish to manifest my will to facilitate their ecclesial communion by means of the necessary measures to guarantee respect for their rightful aspirations....
>
> I decree the following:
>
> a) *A Commission* is instituted for the purpose of facilitating full ecclesial communion of priests, seminarians, religious communities or individuals until now linked in various ways to the Fraternity founded by Mons. Lefebvre, who may wish to remain united to the successor of Peter in the Catholic Church, while preserving their spiritual and liturgical traditions....
> c) Moreover, respect must everywhere be shown for the feelings of all those who are attached to the Latin liturgical tradition by a wide and generous application of the directives already issued some time ago by the Apostolic See for the use of the Roman Missal according to the typical edition of 1962. (nn. 5–6)[87]

(What has since occurred—on January 24, 2009—was the lifting of the excommunication of the four bishops ordained by Archbishop Lefebvre. What remains to be seen even now is whether the greater use of the Tridentine Mass and this lifting of the excommunication results in the healing of the schism so obviously desired by these two recent popes. Clearly the agenda for reconciliation includes acceptance by the followers of Archbishop Lefebvre of the contents and teaching of the documents of Vatican II.)

Stage 3: The *motu proprio* and the accompanying letter of Pope Benedict XVI of July 2007 were issued in which he repeats the progression of the former "publics" for whom this permission was originally intended. But he added a new "public"—those seeking transcendence, specifically the young.[88]

What is of particular note is that the letter states that the two forms of the Roman Mass, the one termed the "ordinary" and the other the "extraordinary" form of the Roman rite, "can be mutually enriching."[89] The issue of what "mutual enrichment" means is not defined. With regard to liturgical forms and practices, this could easily mean the scripture readings or the feasts celebrated. Questions here would be, "Who decides?" and "On what basis or principle?" The other thing that the document cites repeatedly is the value of participation in the liturgy, so much so that the pope envisions that the extraordinary form would be celebrated relatively infrequently. The emphasis placed on "full, conscious, and active participation" in the liturgy is not to be lost when implementing the extraordinary form of the Roman Mass. Put differently, some have sounded the alarm that celebrating the Tridentine Mass is about "going back" to not participating, but, in fact, that is not at all what the document says. Full, conscious, and active participation as required by the celebration of the liturgy will now require knowledge of Latin.

VERBUM DOMINI—POSTSYNODAL APOSTOLIC EXHORTATION OF POPE BENEDICT XVI (2010)

Not unlike his *Sacramentum Caritatis*, Benedict XVI's postsynodal exhortation is also divided into three parts, draws copiously on documents of the church fathers and the magisterium, and reiterates many of the salient points of his pontificate. The document's three parts are titled:

"Verbum Dei"
"Verbum in Ecclesia"
"Verbum Mundo"

The first part is largely concerned with an extended exploration of the proper interpretation of the word of God, one that goes beyond any "scientific" or lexical interpretation without theological (especially paschal and ecclesiological) perspectives brought to bear on the sacred texts under the inspiration of the Holy Spirit. For example, the pope states that "just as the word of God comes to us in the body of Christ, in his Eucharistic body and in the body of the Scriptures, through the working of the Holy Spirit, so too it can only be truly received and understood through that same Spirit" (n. 16).[90]

The most extensive treatment of the importance of the word of God in the liturgy is in the second part (*Verbum in Ecclesia*, nn. 52–70), which calls the liturgy "the privileged setting for the word of God" (n. 52). Several quotations from the Constitution on the Sacred Liturgy (e.g., n. 7 on the presence of Christ in the Liturgy), the Order for the Readings at Mass, and the *Catechism of the Catholic Church* (specifically nn. 1373–74) are used to bolster the important assertions about the theological value of the liturgical proclamation of the word, including those about the intrinsic relationship between the proclamation of the word and the sacrament and the "performative character" of the word. The pope asserts:

> The relationship between word and sacramental gesture is the liturgical expression of God's activity in the history of salvation through the *performative character* of the word itself. In

salvation history there is no separation between what God *says* and what he *does*. His word appears as alive and active (cf. *Heb* 4:12), as the Hebrew term *dabar* itself makes clear. In the liturgical action too, we encounter his word which accomplishes what it says. By educating the People of God to discover the performative character of God's word in the liturgy, we will help them to recognize his activity in salvation history and in their individual lives. (n. 53)

One can only welcome this important emphasis, which can place in proper context the legitimate emphasis more often accorded the educative and informational aspect of the word. A "performative" emphasis restores the word to its role in creation (Gen 1:1) and in the incarnation (John 1:1–14, which text frames the first part of this document).

Coupled with this is the emphasis placed on the sets of lectionary readings assigned to the sacraments that are both liturgically normative and theologically normative as well (n. 52, 57). Relying on the *Catechism*, he states:

> The sacramentality of the word can thus be understood by analogy with the real presence of Christ under the appearances of the consecrated bread and wine. By approaching the altar and partaking in the Eucharistic banquet we truly share in the body and blood of Christ. The proclamation of God's word at the celebration entails an acknowledgment that Christ himself is present, that he speaks to us, and that he wishes to be heard. Saint Jerome speaks of the way we ought to approach both the Eucharist and the word of God: "We are reading the sacred Scriptures. For me, the Gospel is the Body of Christ; for me, the holy Scriptures are his teaching. And when he says: *whoever does not eat my flesh and drink my blood* (*Jn* 6:53), even though these words can also be understood of the [Eucharistic] Mystery, Christ's body and blood are really the word of Scripture, God's teaching. (n. 56)

While much of this section of the document concerns the Eucharist, the explicit references to the proclamation of the word in the

Liturgy of the Hours (n. 62), as well as in the "sacraments of healing"—reconciliation and the anointing of the sick (n. 61)—are extremely important. That all the post–Vatican II sacramental rituals contain elaborate lectionaries for the respective sacraments is a theological statement about the value of the proclamation of the scriptures in sacramental liturgy. When it comes to discussing the liturgy of the word, the pope not only emphasizes the use of the *Book of the Gospels* in the celebration of the liturgy (n. 67), but also stresses that "it is good that the book which contains the word of God should enjoy a visible place of honour inside the Christian temple, without prejudice to the central place proper to the tabernacle containing the Blessed Sacrament" (n. 68).[91] Again one can see here the theological significance that the pope places on the signs and gestures of the liturgy.

While there are obvious ecumenical implications contained in the theology of the word expressed in this document, the pope explicitly refers to the value of the post–Vatican II Lectionary for Sunday Mass as something shared by many Western non–Roman Catholic Christian churches (n. 57), and he also has a rather extensive section on the Bible and ecumenism (n. 46). It is not surprising that a skilled and trained theologian like Pope Benedict XVI treats "the importance of the homily" rather extensively (nn. 59–60) to the point of inviting national episcopal conferences to draft their own directory on homiletics.[92]

Unquestionably this apostolic exhortation both deepens what has been said about the proclamation of the word and about the presence of Christ in the word since *Sacrosanctum Concilium*, which itself was a watershed text given the preceding four centuries of post-Tridentine church life and magisterial apologetics. One can only hope that theologians will take up the insights offered here by the pope and probe even more fully their implications, particularly concerning the performative character of the proclaimed word.

CONCLUSION

From the sixteenth century to the middle of the twentieth century —that is, from the Council of Trent to the pontificate of Pius XII—the

Roman Catholic magisterium has been concerned to clarify and to reassert, among other things, that Christ has an enduring presence in the Eucharist, that in the Mass a sacrifice is offered, that the sacrifice is offered by an ordained priest, and that the laity take part in the Mass not passively but as offerers of the sacrifice. At times those assertions took the form of statements from the Council of Trent that Catholics must believe. At other times the statements came from encyclicals and letters that nevertheless carried the same theological weight. From the mid-1960s onward, beginning with the documents of the Second Vatican Council, the emphasis shifted markedly beyond the sixteenth-century parameters and included aspects of Christ's presence that were long neglected—for example, his presence in the gathered assembly and in the proclaimed word. *Sacrosanctum Concilium* ushered in a whole new era of liturgical forms, participation, and prayer. It remains to be seen whether the latest *motu proprio* allowing a more frequent use of the Tridentine Mass will, in fact, heal the schism within Catholicism caused by the Lefebvrites. It also remains to be seen whether this document and other papal initiatives in the celebration of the liturgy will continue to foster the ideals and prospects laid out in *Sacrosanctum Concilium* for the restoration of the Roman Catholic Mass and for the renewal of church life envisioned in that document (n. 1).

While apostolic exhortations do not share the theological weight of conciliar documents, it is to be welcomed that both of those issued by Pope Benedict XVI are so rich in theology and so insightful for pastoral practice. No other pope has ever fleshed out the relationship among *lex orandi*, *lex credendi*, and *lex agendi* (or *vivendi*) the way this pope has done. That the preaching of the word has become increasingly important in contemporary Roman Catholic theology and liturgical practice is itself a remarkable shift filled with pastoral and ecumenical consequences. Pope Benedict's postsynodal exhortations will likely stand as among his most enduring theological and pastoral legacies.

Chapter Two

Toward a Contemporary Theology of the Eucharist in Light of the Magisterium

In light of what I argued in chapter 1, I will now offer some thoughts about seven concepts that, taken together, can contribute to shaping a contemporary theology of the Eucharist in light of the magisterium.[1]

1. A SACRIFICIAL SACRAMENT[2]

One of the most compelling and frequently reiterated images used by the magisterium about the Eucharist since Trent is that of sacrifice. The sacrificial aspect of the eucharistic mystery was clearly central to the debates at Trent and has been a hallmark in all subsequent magisterial teaching. At times the emphasis is placed on participating in the sacrifice of Christ. At other times the assertion is made that the Eucharist is a sacrifice. The following ideas about "liturgical time" should be kept in mind when trying to comprehend what the eucharistic sacrifice means and is.

NOTIONS OF TIME

We are accustomed to chronological time: such and such happened at a particular time and place, or we look forward to events that we can predict will happen in historical/chronological time. For example, we know that New Year's Day occurs on January 1 and that Thanksgiving Day in the United States is on the fourth Thursday of November.

Obviously we bring this chronological notion of time to our exploration of when Christ died and rose and where it happened. That we can locate the Basilica of the Holy Sepulchre in Jerusalem as the place of Calvary and the empty tomb and that we can revere these as the holiest of holy places is clear. That pilgrims have gone there from the time of Constantine to this day for pilgrimage and prayer is a major facet of our devotional and liturgical life.

At the same time, the death and resurrection of Christ is, by its nature, both something that took place in historical time and also something that transcends chronology, perdures to this day, and will do so until the second coming. This is to say that Christ's sacrifice was accomplished once for all in chronological time and yet, at the same time, is what we can participate in here and now, again and again, until the second coming. This is a liturgical variation on the "already" and "not yet." We believe and know that all Christ accomplished for our salvation, redemption, and sanctification has "already" been accomplished. What has "not yet" happened is the end of time, when chronological time will have come to an end and we will have met the Lord face to face in the kingdom of heaven. In the meantime, we celebrate this "sacrificial sacrament" in our own time, day in, day out.

NOTIONS OF MEMORIAL

Behind these assertions about time is the Jewish notion of memorial that undergirds all our liturgical practice and theology. While the phrase *memorial service* as used today often means a ceremony after someone's death to recall the person and his or her accomplishments, the notion of "memorial" in biblical religion and in the liturgy derived from the Bible is far richer. For that we return to the Book of Exodus. The Passover ritual was and is a communal experience of what was accomplished in the original exodus from Egypt and in any exodus experience today: liberation, freedom, redemption. Similarly, in the eucharistic liturgy, what seems to be separate and separable—past, present, and future—is combined here and now into our experience of all that Christ was, is, and forever will be as savior and redeemer. The Greek term *anamnesis* captures this and has been used to describe the Eucharist as memorial. The "Mystery of Faith" acclamations in the reformed liturgy since Vatican II are particular instances in which the paschal mystery is proclaimed, just prior to the "memorial" section of the Eucharistic prayer.[3]

In addition, the biblical and liturgical notion of "memorial" means that believers participate—literally, *take part in*—what is commemorated through the liturgy. In a sense the phrase *liturgical participation* is redundant, simply because it is integral to the liturgy that we take part in these sacred mysteries until sacraments are no longer necessary and we enjoy their fulfillment in the heavenly liturgy; as we say at the invitation to communion at Mass, "Blessed are those called to the supper of the Lamb." That is one of the goals of communion: to experience its fulfillment forever.

NOTIONS OF SACRIFICE

The term *sacrifice* is clearly a multifaceted reality. Parents regularly sacrifice for their children, for example, in terms of money, time, and attention. Some people sacrifice a kidney so that someone else can live. In the world of biblical religion, *sacrifice* is used for what humans offer (back) to God, whether the fruit of the earth or animals. But here the offering is not simply the giving up of produce or the slaughtering of animals but the motivation and attitude that accompany them. Among the ways in which Catholic theology describes and the liturgy enacts the sacrifice of Christ is that his passion was accomplished once and for all and that in the Eucharist we offer that same sacrifice back to God the Father. Christ dies no more, says St. Paul. What we offer to the Father in heaven through the Eucharist is the risen and ascended Lord. The words of the Roman Canon ring true: "We offer you this sacrifice of praise...."

2. A SACRAMENTAL SACRIFICE[4]

Another way to understand the properly sacrificial dimension of the Eucharist is to use the phrase *sacrificial sacrament*, emphasizing the word *sacrament*. This is to say that the Eucharist, when compared with the other six sacraments, is very much like them and yet also unique.

From as early as the thirteenth century, when Peter Lombard listed the seven sacraments, the Eucharist was among them. That it is one of the seven sacraments of the church has been reiterated time and again. The fact that it has been called one of the two "major" sacraments along with baptism because of clear biblical evidence for them has been ecumenically beneficial. That the Eucharist is one of the seven numbered sacraments is a staple of Catholic theology and practice.

The Eucharist is also a particular sacrament, because in our theological and liturgical tradition it is argued that all the sacraments lead to or derive from the Eucharist. While medieval commentaries have differed about how this is the case, at least it can be asserted that baptism and confirmation lead to the Eucharist: these three sacraments, taken together, are the sacraments of Christian initiation. The forgiveness of sins in the sacrament of penance and the anointing of the sick return us to the eucharistic altar. (One who was "excommunicated" by serious sin in the early church was reconciled through penance to the Eucharist.) At ordination the priest is given the power and responsibility to celebrate the Eucharist and thereby to offer sacrifice. The celebration of marriage, especially at a Nuptial Mass, reflects the intimacy of Christ and his church mirrored in the married life.

The priority thus placed on the Eucharist in the West was accompanied by a diminished role for the Liturgy of the Hours in the daily liturgical life of most Catholics.[5] This led to an almost exclusive emphasis on the Eucharist as *the* liturgy of the church. That we are recovering a wider notion of liturgy as encompassing all the sacraments and all other liturgies is important. That more and more people avail themselves of opportunities to participate in the celebration of the daily Hours is impressive and theologically important. All of this helps to contextualize, but not to eclipse, the Eucharist as the sacrament of sacraments.

This is at least part of the reason why *Lumen Gentium* (n. 11) will assert that the faithful, by virtue of their baptismal priesthood, "take part in the Eucharistic sacrifice, which is the fount and apex of the whole Christian life, they offer the Divine Victim to God, and offer themselves along with It."[6] The phrase *fount and apex* (otherwise translated as "summit and source") is important and strong theological language to describe both participation and the eucharistic sacrifice—the "sacrament of sacraments."

3. A PERMANENT PRESENCE

That "real presence" and variations on this phrase have been a hallmark of Catholic doctrine on the Eucharist since before the Council of Trent is clear. That Christ is "really, corporeally" present under the forms of bread and wine is classic Catholic theological teaching and catechetical instruction. That the real presence of Christ in the Eucharist is permanent makes it unique in the constellation that comprises the seven sacraments. After the consecration, bread and wine are irrevocably changed into the body and blood of Christ. Therefore, after the celebration of the Eucharist whatever elements remain do, in fact, remain what they've become.

From the instruction of Pope Benedict XIV in the eighteenth century up to the latest *General Instruction of the Roman Missal (GIRM)*, there is the clear direction that the eucharistic elements given in communion should be consecrated at the same Mass. The rationale behind Pope Benedict's admonition was that if only the priest received communion consecrated at that Mass and the communicants (however many there were) were to receive instead communion from the sacrament reserved in the tabernacle, it would give the impression that the sacrifice at Mass was separate from the sacrament in the tabernacle. Pope Benedict saw this as separating what is inseparable: sacrifice and sacrament. They are part of the same reality and should be experienced, revered, and taught to be such. True, some would argue that the giving of communion from the tabernacle at Mass shows that one Mass continues to another and will do so until the end of time. Therefore, this is perceived to be a sign of continuity. In fact, however, the liturgical practice of giving communion from hosts consecrated at that Mass shows an inner consistency emphasizing the importance of the liturgy as a particular event in which priest-presider and the rest of the assembly participate. Communion for both from the same altar matters.

The way the liturgy of the Eucharist reflects the principle of continuity—that one Mass leads to the next until the end of time—is reflected elsewhere, namely, in the dropping of a piece of the broken eucharistic bread into the chalice. This comes from two ancient practices. The first is the *fermentum*, whereby a portion of the consecrated bread from the pope's Mass was taken by deacons to other churches in Rome and placed in the chalice to show the unity of the papal Eucharist with the rest of the liturgies in the city. The second practice is the *sancta*, whereby the priest would leave on the altar a piece of the consecrated bread from the Mass he is celebrating and place the piece of consecrated bread on the altar from the preceding Mass into the chalice. This showed the continuity of one Mass to the next.

At the same time, it is clear that the Eucharist has always been reserved after Mass as well. This is because of the need for the church to have it available for those who cannot come to the assembly to celebrate the Eucharist, largely because of poor health. Historically this practice of eucharistic reservation led to the worship and adoration of the Eucharist.[7] What the Eastern liturgical tradition calls "holy things for holy people" deserves reverence when kept after the liturgy. The present *GIRM* indicates that the tabernacle for the reserved sacrament should not be on the altar on which the Eucharist is celebrated, that it should be either in the sanctuary apart from where the liturgy is celebrated or in a separate chapel, and that an oil lamp or candle should mark where the tabernacle is located.[8]

All of this is to suggest that the presence of Christ in the Eucharist after the consecration is real, abiding, and permanent. These practices reflect the doctrine of the "real presence."

4. WORSHIP OF THE EUCHARIST OUTSIDE OF MASS

The practice of showing reverence for the reserved species developed over time and has had a respected place in the faith and devotional lives of Catholics. That this reverence is seen to compliment and not to derogate in any way from the celebration of the liturgy is reiterated in all documents governing its various forms, such as processions, exposition, and benediction.[9] Again, it is clear that the first rationale for reservation was communion outside of Mass. More recently, another reason why hosts are reserved in tabernacles is to satisfy the sacramental hunger caused by those situations in which a Mass cannot be celebrated, and communion is thus distributed according to either the special Sunday[10] or weekday[11] rites without a priest.

A number of practices centered on the reserved Eucharist existed prior to Vatican II and were regarded not as liturgy. After Vatican II, a ritual book from the Congregation for Divine Worship was published entitled *Worship of the Eucharist Outside of Mass*. This book governs all such practices. Its introduction is especially instructive about the relationship between such practices and the celebration of Mass. In effect, this document envisions that the reserved sacrament be exposed in a monstrance (from the Latin word *monstrare*, "to show") or in a ciborium, the vessel from which the eucharistic bread is distributed. This latter option reflects in a graphic way the intrinsic relationship between communion and worship of the Eucharist outside of Mass. These celebrations also involve a liturgy of the word, again a liturgical way of reflecting the structure and liturgical priority of the celebration of the Mass itself.

The lament of some of the papal magisterium about the neglect of the worship of the Eucharist outside of Mass has been met by an increase in these practices. In this regard Pope Benedict XVI's example of conducting such services at recent World Youth Days is graphic and demonstrable. That they were met with incredible silence by the tens of thousands in attendance is remarkable. This papal initiative reflects pastoral initiatives on almost all levels of church life, which, in turn, reflect an increase in their frequency and popularity. There is legitimate debate about their place in the repertoire of liturgical and devotional practices in the life of a parish or other liturgical community. Among the reasons why these celebrations outside of Mass are thought to be popular are two: objectivity and silence.

Allow me to recount my personal experience of Sunday Mass and Monday devotions when I was in grammar school and growing up in the American Catholicism of the 1950s. Participating in Sunday Mass or in Sunday services was a sine qua non for all of us who lived in what today would be called a multicultural neighborhood. Catholics went to Mass, and we who were in the parish school attended the "children's Mass." We sat in the front of the church with our classmates, and the teachers took attendance. On most Sundays we sang four hymns, listened to a sermon directed to us children, and almost always received communion. We followed the rest of the Mass by reading Missals and were otherwise silent. After Mass we remained for a few moments of silent prayer and then were dismissed row by row. Because I was an altar server, on Monday evenings I took my turn at serving the Miraculous Medal devotion and benediction. At that service we sang the opening hymn, said the novena prayers along with the priest, and listened to his sermon. We servers then prepared the altar for the exposition of the consecrated host in the monstrance by the priest. After he did this, the priest came to the bottom of the steps to meet the servers who held the thurible with burning charcoal and the boat with the incense, which the priest then combined so that he could incense the monstrance. This was followed by singing (in Latin) the Collect from the Mass for the Solemnity of Corpus Christi. The priest then ascended the altar and, wearing a special vestment called the humeral veil, raised the monstrance, faced the assembly, and used the monstrance to make the Sign of the Cross over us. He then returned the monstrance to the altar. He descended the altar steps, removed the humeral veil, and led the congregation in saying the Divine Praises. He then returned the consecrated host to the tabernacle, descended the altar stairs, and led us in singing "Holy God, We Praise Thy Name."

This was standard fare in suburban Catholicism outside New York City, but it was also replicated with some variations throughout the country.

My point in recounting this in detail is to show how we participated in Sunday Mass largely by watching and listening, while at Monday night devotions we participated fully throughout the service by singing and praying the same prayers in unison (and by heart). The incense was required and added to the solemnity of the devotions. I wonder whether the felt need for participation that we experienced at novenas in the preconciliar church is now met in regular celebration of the Sunday liturgy, and whether the felt need for objectivity and silence that was formerly experienced at the liturgy is now met at eucharistic adoration services outside of Mass.

For me, a key issue is silence, especially on college campuses. At Catholic University we celebrate Mass three times daily in the main chapel on campus. On Wednesday and Thursday evenings we have variations on eucharistic adoration outside of Mass, with a "Praise and Worship" service on Wednesdays and a variation on exposition of the Blessed Sacrament and Compline on Thursdays. These services are packed. Masses are not. One of my suspicions is that the students crave silence, even in an IM, text-message, cell-phone world.

Theologically these services derive from the reality of Christ's permanent and enduring presence in the eucharistic species after the celebration of Mass.

5. FREQUENCY

The clear directive in the contemporary magisterium is that priests should celebrate Mass daily in order to offer the faithful the opportunity to attend and participate regularly. However, several current conditions need to be kept in mind that affect whether this ideal can be realized today; among them are the decline in the number of ordained priests and the responsibility that some priests now have to celebrate Mass in several locations, especially on Sundays.

The issue of frequency of the Eucharist on the priest's part is related to other concerns, many of which have been brought to my attention by priests in clergy conferences and which, in turn, have been the impetus for very fruitful discussions among the assembled clergy about the variety of circumstances in which they preside at the Eucharist, such as nursing homes, prisons, and schools, and the variety of demands placed upon them in these liturgical contexts. I will offer thoughts on three of these concerns and will then follow this with some pastoral applications.

1. *The role of the presiding priest in the post–Vatican II liturgy and the demands it makes upon him.* The esteemed British historian Eamon Duffy has indicated that the present rite lacks objectivity and a structured form that allows the priest-presider to be engaged in this unique act of prayer without being unnecessarily attentive to the need to choose from a number of options: for example, which saint to commemorate; which Penitential Rite, Preface, and Eucharistic prayer to pray; which intercessions to choose; what songs to sing at the entrance and communion processions; whether to preach and what. I have raised this matter for discussion at clergy days, and some parish priests reply that while they can appreciate these concerns they judge that the daily scripture readings offer them the material for their daily *lectio divina* and that the study of commentaries and praying over these texts is a great stimulus to their spiritual lives. For monks and mendicants, this issue is mitigated by daily eucharistic concelebration of the conventual Mass. These and issues like it are important to factor into the possibility of priest "presiding fatigue."

2. *The structure of the Order of Mass.* The fact that we have one Order of Mass in the revised Mass is a marked change from the previous Tridentine Missal, which had three forms: Low Mass, High Mass, and Solemn High Mass. Given that we now have one structure, the (parish) priest often finds himself in a position to choose from a number of options to simplify the celebration on weekdays: for example, to eliminate music despite the fact that the Order of Mass explicitly calls for music at every celebration and a certain hierarchy for what to sing is indicated in the USCCB document *Sing to the Lord: Music in Divine Worship* (2007). As early as the 1980s Father Anscar Chupungco, a respected authority on liturgy and former professor at Sant'Anselmo, argued for a "ferial Order of Mass," which was a much simpler form of the Order of Mass designed for daily use.[12]

3. *The number of Masses in different settings.* It is not uncommon for the (parish) priest to celebrate Masses in more than one location— for example, the parish church, school, hospital, nursing home, or prison. This requires that he be flexible and that he travel to several sites. It is a variation on the concern about the number of Masses some

priests celebrate on a weekend. While the multiplicity of Masses attests to people's desire to celebrate and participate in the Mass, for the priest there can be an overload in terms of the burdens that these multiple Masses place upon him.

The daily celebration of the Eucharist has traditionally been urged as a baseline of priestly formation and the priestly life. Indeed, the Eucharist is "source and font" of the Christian, not to say the priestly life. But a number of factors have influenced (parish) priests to devise strategies so that overload and "eucharistic burnout" does not occur. Conversations about this phenomenon at clergy in-service days are always spirited, thoughtful, and respectful of the church's tradition and teaching.

A few years ago I met a former student from Theological College who now serves as pastor of three parishes. He recounted that on Sunday morning he leaves his home dressed in Mass vestments at 7 a.m. and drives to the first of four places at which he will celebrate Sunday Mass, with the expectation that he will return home, still vested, at 3 p.m., thoroughly exhausted. And these Sunday celebrations are preceded on Saturday with confessions in one of the churches and a Saturday evening Mass. A few years before that, I delivered some lectures in the Pacific Northwest where, again, I met a former student. He recounted that on any given Saturday he starts his weekend Mass journey by flying to two islands to celebrate Mass at each location and then, on Sunday, drives to three churches where he celebrates Mass in succession. As I write this chapter, the archbishop of Liverpool, England, has commissioned twenty-two laypeople to preside at funerals in the absence of priests.[13] This caused serious debate about a number of issues, including the desirability of having this kind of service replace a Funeral Mass; the proper role of the ordained priest at the time of bereavement; the role of the church at a time when many who do not regularly practice the faith return at their time of grief but cannot engage a priest; and the roles of the ordained and lay leaders in pastoral life in the church today.[14] The practice of countries—in parts of Africa, for example—in which priests travel long distances to celebrate sacraments a few times a year means that laity lead parts of the funeral rite and burial, and then there is a Mass for all the deceased when the priest can be there to preside.

Some will argue historically and sociologically that the regular celebration of the sacraments and the availability of numbers of priests to celebrate them was a comparatively recent phenomenon in America, and that therefore our working out strategies today to accommodate new pastoral circumstances is really a return to the way it had been, with the faith handed on by the lay faithful and sustained by regular prayer meetings that were not sacraments.[15] This data does and should factor into discussions of pastoral planning and practice. Yet, there is the immediate (and hard) reality that expectations are there and sometimes it is at funerals and weddings that pastors and pastoral practice can be harshly judged.

The presumption that all funerals will be Masses and that a couple can always celebrate their wedding at a nuptial Mass is being challenged in practice in many American dioceses today, simply because of the decline in the number of priests and the consolidation of parishes. It is common in some parishes that funerals take the place of the (one) regularly scheduled daily Eucharist. This calls into question the place of the Eucharist in the three stages of the funeral rite—vigil, Eucharist, committal. The reformed *Order of Christian Funerals* envisions all three. I would argue that this allows for placing emphasis on grief and the individual who is deceased at the vigil (with any eulogies done at this service), and then emphasis on our incorporation (including that of the deceased) into the paschal mystery in a unique way at the Eucharist.

The possibility that a wedding may not be at a nuptial Mass can mean that a couple is offered the opportunity to have their wedding take place at a regularly scheduled Sunday Eucharist, similar to what happens when baptisms are celebrated at Sunday Mass. This can be a real stretch for some couples who request a church wedding. On the one hand, it might mitigate some of the extremes of wedding preparation that are focused only on the bride and groom and invited guests to the exclusion of the parish community, which should be the locus of the couple's faith life and journey. Issues of ecclesiology and church belonging loom large here. At the same time, the inability to celebrate

a Mass can be a useful thing for an ecumenical wedding at which significant numbers of anticipated attendees would not be able to partake
in communion. At such celebrations of the word and vows, a permanent deacon can preside; this would offer them a role and responsibility for their ordained ministry to flourish.

I suspect that these examples are only the tip of the iceberg of
the pastoral realities that pastors deal with regularly. The liturgical/
theological issue that remains at stake is: What is the role of the celebration of the Eucharist at funerals and weddings? My own sense is
that we Catholics do funerals right, according to the reformed *Order of
Christian Funerals*. I do, however, wonder whether the Eucharist might
be getting lost at some weddings for some couples whose expectations
and planning are not really eucharistically focused.

The publication in the United States of the ritual *Sunday
Celebrations in the Absence of a Priest* offers the structure for a Liturgy of
the Word (or the celebration of the Hours) with communion when a
priest is not available for Mass. On weekdays the rite for the distribution of communion outside of Mass is offered as an alternative for daily
Eucharist. The more recent papal magisterium (from Pope John Paul II
on) clearly distinguishes these practices from the celebration of the
Eucharist and notes their "sacramental incompleteness."[16] This is an
important issue of eucharistic theology and practice.

Finally, allow me to return to the example with which I began this
section, namely, that of priests regularly presiding at several Masses on
a weekend. For many priests this causes eucharistic burnout, not in the
sense of not desiring the Eucharist, but that such frequent celebrations
result in a certain weariness and lack of attention to what one is actually doing toward the end of those Sundays. There is wisdom in the
provisions of canon law about the number of Masses a priest should
celebrate on any given day. But pastoral necessities often trump the law.

6. A VISIBLE WORD

Certainly one of the great revolutions to have taken place in the
contemporary reform of the liturgy has been the emphasis placed on

the proclamation of the scriptures at all liturgies, especially at the Eucharist. From noting that Christ is present in the proclaimed word in the *Sacrosanctum Concilium*, through the Synod on the Word of God in the Life and Mission of the Church, and in the postsynodal exhortation *Verbum Domini*, there is ample evidence of nothing less than a sea change in terms of the emphasis that the scriptures receive in the reformed Catholic liturgy and in Catholic life today.

That the Catholic Church took the initiative in 1970 to produce a three-year lectionary of scripture readings for the Sunday Eucharist and a two-year lectionary of scripture readings for the weekday Eucharist was and is an enormous achievement. That the Sunday cycle of readings has influenced the lectionary structure of many other non–Roman Catholic liturgical churches is nothing short of an ecumenical success story.

In his classic commentary on the Gospel of John, St. Augustine asserts that one joins the word to an element and one has a sacrament, a "visible word." Alternatively, I think one could argue that the Eucharist is an "audible symbol," in the sense that through both proclamation and the enactment of the Eucharist we are joined with the paschal mystery of Christ (understanding that the Greek *symballein* means "to throw together").

The issue I want to raise here is how to understand the Eucharist as one act of worship (as inspired by *Sacrosanctum Concilium*, n. 56). The insightful language about the "two tables" of word and altar can offer a welcome corrective to what had perhaps been an overemphasis on what took place at the altar table—offertory, consecration, and communion—with a resulting eclipse of the proclamation of the word (although such proclamation was always a part of the Catholic liturgy of the Eucharist). Yet, in practice sometimes we still refer to what happens at the altar as *the* Eucharist without noting that the word is intrinsic. That the rite of communion contains an echo of the proclamation of the word is evident from the fact that the communion antiphons are almost always taken from the scriptures and sometimes (on seasonal Sundays) from the gospel of the day. My own sense is that when homilies at the Sunday Eucharist regularly refer to moving from word to altar (and why this is done), this (perhaps subtle reference on a regular basis) can go a long way toward fulfilling the conciliar teaching that the Eucharist is one act of worship (*Sacrosanctum Concilium*, n. 56). It is indeed a "visible word."

7. JEWEL IN THE CROWN OF CATHOLICISM

My own sense is that "Jewel in the Crown of Catholicism" is a particularly apt way to describe the Eucharist as a precious gift to the church. When viewed from different angles and through different lenses, a jewel's many facets and contours can be seen. A true jewel is a visually inexhaustible treasure. The Eucharist is an inexhaustible treasure theologically and spiritually.

The celebration of the Eucharist is based on the sacramental principle, derived from the Incarnation, that we experience God in the liturgy through the use of human means of communication (words, gestures, movement, persons) and the things of this earth (bread and wine). Each of these, in turn, could be developed into being a part of the theology of the Eucharist. (For example, we experience God in and among one another as the gathered assembly hierarchically ordered and enacted through the ministries of a variety of people presided over by the ordained priest.) But the particularity of the Eucharist would have us focus on the very manufacture of the bread and wine, which reflects Catholicism's valuing and revering of human ingenuity and human work. At the same time, the human substratum of dining together on which the Eucharist is based may well need a lot of shoring up in practice. Studies show that there is a decided decline in the opportunities for numerous American families both to dine together and to prepare the meal that is shared. Some studies have produced evidence that many American families rarely eat meals together. While it may be naive to try to imitate the emphasis that some ethnic groups, such as Italians and Chinese, place on food and dining together in an American context, much can be lost when such an experience is regarded as rare. But dining is also what is particular to the sacrament of the Eucharist as distinct from the other sacraments. It deserves priority and emphasis.

An intrinsic connection exists between bread and wine offered as "the work of human hands" and the Eucharist as the celebration of "the work of our redemption." My own sense is that in an increasingly environmentally conscious culture, the Eucharist as based on creation can be a very fruitful avenue to explore when trying to explain it theologically. We can and do experience God in nature and creation, especially when we reflect on them as God's gifts to us. In the Eucharist we can view the baking of bread and the fermenting of wine as paschal processes of dying. The end result is bread and wine, consecrated to become the body and blood of Christ, and it is through these sacred elements that we participate in the paschal mystery of Christ. And when we are sent forth from the Eucharist we return to the world of everyday life to love and serve the Lord, having been loved and served by the Lord in and by the Eucharist.

It is all of a piece—or should be. In this sense the Eucharist is integral to and integrative of the Christian life. The jewel in the crown of Catholicism indeed!

Chapter Three

What the Magisterium Says about the Ordained Priesthood

The documents to be reviewed here are from the canons, decrees, and teachings of the Council of Trent (1545–63); the Constitution on the Sacred Liturgy (*Sacrosanctum Concilium*, 1963); the Constitution on the Church (*Lumen Gentium*, 1964); the Constitution on Divine Revelation (*Dei Verbum*, 1965); the Decree on the Pastoral Office of Bishops in the Church (*Christus Dominus*, 1965); the Decree on Priestly Formation (*Optatam Totius*, 1965); the Decree on the Ministry and Life of Priests/Presbyters (*Presbyterorum Ordinis*, 1965); the Declaration on the Admission of Women to the Ministerial Priesthood from the Congregation for the Doctrine of the Faith (*Inter Insigniores*, 1976); Pope John Paul II's letter On the Mystery and Worship of the Eucharist (*Dominicae Cenae*, 1980); selections from the *Catechism of the Catholic Church* (1992); the postsynodal exhortation *Pastores Dabo Vobis* (1992); the apostolic letter On the Ordination of Women (*Ordinatio Sacerdotalis*, 1994); the encyclical *Ecclesia de Eucharistia* (2003); and the postsynodal exhortations *Sacramentum Caritatis* (2007) and *Verbum Domini* (2010).

As noted at the beginning of chapter 1, an operative principle in what follows is that in order to understand the contents and import of a church document on a particular topic it is helpful to place it in the context of what was said before it and after it in other documents on the same topic.[1] Because an understanding of the ecclesial, liturgical, and theological background to a particular document is essential to understanding it correctly, this chapter will begin with a discussion of the normative and theologically binding canons and decrees from the Council of Trent on the Orders.

DECREES, CANONS, AND TEACHINGS OF THE COUNCIL OF TRENT

The exposition on the ordained priesthood in the decrees and canons of the Council of Trent is derived from a number of its documents spanning from 1547 to 1563. The number of assertions and the length of time it took to develop them are important to note. They include the Decree on Reform (Session 5, June 1546); the Decree and Canons on Sacraments (Session 7, March 1547); the Decree and Canons on the Most Holy Sacrament of the Eucharist (Session 13, October 1551); the Teaching and Canons concerning the Most Holy Sacraments of Penance and Last Anointing (Session 14, November 1551); the Teaching and Canons on the Most Holy Sacrifice of the Mass (Session 22, September 1562); and the Decree and Canons concerning the True and Catholic Doctrine of the Sacrament of Order, to Condemn the Errors of Our Time (Session 23, July 1563).[2]

The first decree on sacraments (in general) reflects what was stated at Trent's very opening, that among its aims was "the removal of errors and the rooting out of heresies which have arisen at the present time concerning the most holy sacraments...."[3] It is no wonder, then, that Piet Fransen will astutely observe:

> [T]he assembled Fathers never delineate a *complete* exposition of the doctrine of the sacraments....[T]hey aimed only at condemning the heretical positions of the Lutherans and the Calvinists, deliberately dropping whatever question, however important, was still under discussion among Catholic theologians....[T]he positive Catholic doctrine in the decrees and canons is therefore on the *necessary minimum*, in opposition and contrast to the heretical positions of that time.[4]

In effect, the assertions of Trent are best understood when they are regarded as laconic, specific, reactive, and open-ended (as noted in chapter 1).

My concern will be to summarize what the fathers at Trent said about the ordained priest/presbyter. Two distinctions should be kept in mind. First (recalling what was said in chapter 1) is the distinction between decrees and canons: the latter asserts what Catholics must believe about the sacrament of order and the former summarizes additional magisterial information about the priesthood. The second distinction concerns the use of the Latin term *sacerdos* and *presbyter* in these and subsequent church documents. (I regret that in several English translations the word *priest* is often used to translate both Latin terms, and for the term *pastoralis*, or variations on it, the word *pastor* is used. In what follows, I will make the necessary changes in those translations to reflect as precisely as possible what these texts say. This will be especially important where reference is made to Christ the High Priest [*sacerdos*] and his unique mediation, the ordained priest as offerer of sacrifice [*sacerdos*], and the presbyter as a member of the college of presbyters [*presbyteris*].)

DECREE ON REFORM

The assertions about *preaching* in the Decree on Reform are very important and should be borne in mind as we evaluate the assertions on preaching in the documents of Vatican II and subsequent magisterial teachings. The Tridentine decree states that

> since the preaching of the gospel is no less necessary than instruction for a Christian state, and thus the chief task of the bishops, the same holy council has decided that all bishops, archbishops, primates and all others who preside over the churches are personally bound…to preach the holy gospel of Jesus Christ.[5]

It goes on to say that if those just mentioned cannot fulfill this responsibility, "they shall be bound…to appoint men [*viros*] who are capable of carrying out effectively this duty of preaching":[6]

Archpriests [archpresbyters] also, ordinary priests and any others who have some control over parochial and other churches [*Archipresbyteri quoque plebani et quicumque parochiales*] and have the care of souls, are to feed with the words of salvation the people committed to their charge. This they should do personally or through others who are competent, by teaching at least on Sundays and solemn feasts, according to their own and their hearers' capacity, what is necessary for all to know with a view to salvation, by proclaiming briefly and with ease of expression the vices they must avoid and the virtues they must cultivate....[7]

These charges are followed by instructions about the bishop's responsibility to censure those who do not fulfill this task: "they are to be brought under ecclesiastical or other censures at the discretion of the bishop," and "regulars of any order [*Regulares vero cuiuscunque ordinis*] may not preach even in churches of their own order unless they have been tested and approved by their own superiors...and with that permission they are bound to come in person before the bishops and ask for their blessing before they begin to preach."[8]

DECREE ON THE SACRAMENTS

Canon 9 asserts that "if anyone says that in the three sacraments, namely, baptism, confirmation and order, a character, namely, a spiritual and indelible mark, is not imprinted on the soul, because of which they cannot be repeated, let him be anathema."[9] The term used here is *order* (*ordine*) and does not specify anything more (or less) about the character associated with holy orders.

DECREE ON THE MOST HOLY SACRAMENT OF THE EUCHARIST

This set of decrees and canons contains no explicit reference to the role of the priest in the Eucharist.

TEACHING CONCERNING THE MOST HOLY SACRAMENTS OF PENANCE AND ANOINTING

All references to the priest acting in the sacrament of penance in these decrees use the word *sacerdos*, such as in chapter 2:6.[10] The same is true for canon 9, which mentions the priest (*sacerdos*) twice.[11] When referring to the institution of the sacrament of the last anointing the first chapter refers to the Letter of James (5:14–15), which uses the word *elder* (*presbyter*).[12] When describing the minister of this sacrament, it uses the term *presbyters* (*presbyteros*) twice, as well as *priests* (*sacerdotes*).[13] In canon 4 on the sacrament of the last anointing, the text speaks about "the presbyters of the church who as blessed James enjoins, should be brought in to anoint the sick person" who are "priests [*sacerdotes*] who have been ordained by a bishop...." and that "the proper minister of last anointing is...a priest [*sacerdotum*]."[14]

TEACHING AND CANONS ON THE MOST HOLY SACRIFICE OF THE MASS

Not surprisingly, all the references to the priest at Mass are explicitly to "priest" (*sacerdos*). The first refers to "the one and the same victim here offering himself by the ministry of his priests [*sacerdotum*]"[15] The second exhorts "priests" (*sacerdotibus*) to mix water with the wine at Mass.[16] Canon 2 contains two references to the "priest"; the first asserts that Christ made apostles "priests" (*apostolos sacerdotes*) and that they and "other priests" (*aliique sacerdotes*) are to "offer his body and blood."[17]

THE TRUE AND CATHOLIC DOCTRINE OF THE SACRAMENT OF ORDER, TO CONDEMN THE ERRORS OF OUR TIME

The opening sentence of this section asserts that "sacrifice and priesthood [*sacrificium et sacerdotium*] are so joined together by God's foundation that each exists in every law."[18] The second chapter asserts the existence of orders of ministers "to give official assistance to priests [*qui sacerdotio*]."[19] Chapter 4 repeats the assertion in canon 9 on sacraments in general about the existence of a "character" "in the sacrament of order [*in sacramento ordinis*]."[20] Canons 1 and 2 assert the existence of a "visible and external priesthood [*sacerdotium visibile*]" and observe that "other orders" exist apart from "the priesthood [*praeter sacerdotium*]."[21] Canon 6 asserts that in the Catholic Church a hierarchy exists "consisting of bishops, priests [presbyters] and ministers [*ex episcopis, presbyteris et ministris*]." Canon 7 asserts that bishops are of higher rank than "priests" and that the power of the bishop is not held in common with priests. But what is interesting is that here the Latin *presbyter* is used, not *sacerdos*.[22] In the canons that follow on reform, canon 7 links the bishop with "priests" (*sacerdotibus*).[23] It asserts that one cannot be advanced to the presbyterate (*ad presbyteratus*) before the twenty-fifth year,[24] that those to be advanced to the presbyterate (*ad presbyteratus*) should be men who have conducted themselves devoutly and faithfully in earlier ministries,[25] and that at ordination "presbyters" (*presbyteri*) receive the power to forgive sins, although they must be "priests" (*sacerdotes*) regarded as qualified to do so.[26]

OBSERVATIONS ABOUT TRENT

Any general assertions based on computing the number of times a word is used can be both revealing and misleading, especially when word usages are not uniform. Certainly this is the case when dealing with the assertions of Trent about the ordained priesthood. Recall that Trent did not use either the word *priest* or the word *presbyter* when describing the *importance* of preaching; on the other hand, the assertions about the *role* of the bishop and those with a pastoral responsibility in preaching (archpresbyters and pastors) could not have been stronger. In addition, the prominent position of preaching as one of the essential tasks of the ordained so early on at Trent reflects the importance of always relating ministry with ministers, specifically to delineate a theology of ministry, not (just) of "ministers." Here preaching has an eminent place.

The fact that *sacerdos* language is used frequently in the Tridentine texts asserts the significance of the role of one who offers sacrifice. (Recall here that when describing the ministry of bishop in the patristic era, *sacerdos* most often referred to the bishop as *sacerdos*, the one who offered sacrifice for his flock.) The fact that *presbyter* is also present in the Tridentine documents reveals that "presbyter" language continues to be used despite the polemical context at the time of Trent. It is at least noteworthy that where *presbyter* is used in reference to the last anointing, it is in reference to the evidence from the Letter of James 5:14–15. That "presbyter" language is used in the last decree cited about those to be advanced to the presbyterate reflects the fact that the rites of ordination in the West uniformly refer, not to the "priesthood," but to the "presbyterate." The word *presbyter* is also used immediately prior to this when the hierarchy is listed as bishops, presbyters, and ministers. The use of *presbyter* here reflects the New Testament and early patristic usage that avoids any reference to "priest" as *sacerdos* when it lists or describes those in the ministries we have come to call ordained ministry. The use of the term *order* to refer to the sacramental "character" conferred at ordination may well be deliberate and an effort to sidestep the still then much-disputed issues at Trent about the "powers" of the priesthood and the (exact) meaning of episcopal *consecration*, as opposed to *ordination* to the episcopacy. That a character exists as a result of baptism, confirmation, and ordination is clear, and that it denotes unrepeatability is equally clear.[27] Any further elaboration or delineation remains matter for legitimate debate.[28]

With reference to our specific topic at hand, the theology of ordained priesthood, at least four things can be deduced:

1. Sacerdotal language is often used in relation to how the priest functions when celebrating the sacrifice of the Mass or the sacraments of penance and anointing (understanding that "presbyter" language is also used regarding anointing).
2. Presbyteral language continued to be used in the official magisterial documents from Trent, even when the Catholic Church was under intense scrutiny to defend orthodox teaching against the Reformers, specifically their rejection of the sacrificial nature of the Mass.

3. Little is definitively asserted about sacramental "character" except that it is imprinted and cannot be repeated.
4. At times the relationship of bishops, presbyters, and other ministers is asserted at Trent even though the kind of relationship between and among them that existed in the patristic era had changed because of the church's expansion, as well as the rise of monk priests and mendicant priests who functioned in relation to but often largely in isolation from the diocesan bishop.

ORDAINED PRIESTHOOD IN THE DOCUMENTS OF VATICAN II

Just as it is important to distinguish the canons of the Council of Trent from its decrees (not to mention the catechisms that were written in light of its teachings and to foster their understanding), it is also important to distinguish among genres of council documents: constitutions, decrees, and declarations.[29] Noting that hierarchy of documents, the following are the sources for the assertions of the Second Vatican Council about the ordained priesthood: Dogmatic Constitution on the Church (*Lumen Gentium,* 1964); Dogmatic Constitution on Divine Revelation (*Dei Verbum,* 1965); Constitution on the Sacred Liturgy (*Sacrosanctum Concilium,* 1963); Pastoral Constitution on the Church in the Modern World (*Gaudium et Spes,* 1965); Decree on the Pastoral Office of Bishops in the Church (*Christus Dominus,* 1965); and most specifically, Decree on Priestly Formation (*Optatam Totius,* 1965)[30] and Decree on the Ministry and Life of Priests (*Presbyterorum Ordinis,* 1965).

In describing the presence of Christ in the sacrifice of the Mass, *Sacrosanctum Concilium* refers to the teaching of the Council of Trent and then expands on it by asserting that Christ is present "in the person of the minister—the same [Christ] who then offered himself on the cross is now making his offering through the agency of priests [*idem nunc offerens sacerdotum ministerio*]" (n. 7).[31] This statement stands in direct line with the teaching of Trent, whose immediate theological and polemical context was the teaching of the Reformers, who denied that the Mass is a sacrifice. It goes on to say that Christ's power is present in the sacraments; "thus when anyone baptizes, Christ himself is baptizing" (quoting St. Augustine).[32] The explicit Christology of these assertions should be borne in mind as the Council documents are digested and then reiterated through later documents from the pontificates of John Paul II and Benedict XVI.

LUMEN GENTIUM—DOGMATIC CONSTITUTION ON THE CHURCH (1964)

The teaching of *Lumen Gentium* on the ordained is contextualized within chapter 2 of this constitution, which is titled "On the People of God." Whatever may be asserted from prior magisterial texts or the writings of theologians that describe the ordained as being above the nonordained is reversed here, according to Avery Dulles. He asserts that, with regard to the teaching of Vatican II on the ordained priesthood, "if anything the common priesthood is more exalted, for the ministers are ordained for the sake of service toward the whole people of God."[33]

The key texts of *Lumen Gentium* about the relationship between the ordained and the nonordained are in numbers 10 to 11. Most importantly, the constitution points out that "the common priesthood of the faithful and the ministerial or hierarchical priesthood [*sacerdotium*], though they differ in essence and not simply in degree, are nevertheless interrelated: each in its own particular way shares in the one priesthood of Christ."[34] Both priesthoods take part in and offer the eucharistic sacrifice (n. 11, citing *Mediator Dei*). The constitution asserts:

> On the one hand, the ministerial priest [*Sacerdos quidem ministerialis*], through the sacred power that he enjoys, forms and governs the priestly people; in the person of Christ, he brings about the Eucharistic sacrifice, and offers this to God in the name of all the people. The faithful, on the other hand, by virtue of their royal priesthood join [*populum sacerdotalem efformat et regit*] in the offering of the Eucharist and they exercise their priesthood [*vi regalis sui*

sacerdotii] in receiving the sacraments, in prayer and thanksgiving, through the witness of a holy life, by self-denial and active charity. (n. 10)[35]

In *Lumen Gentium's* next chapter, "On the Hierarchical Structure of the Church," it asserts that "the bishops have undertaken along with their fellow-workers, the priests [*presbyteris*, 'presbyters'] and deacons, the service of the community, presiding in the place of God over the flock" (n. 20).[36] It goes on to say that "in the bishops, therefore, assisted by the priests [*presbyteri*, 'presbyters'], there is present in the midst of believers the Lord Jesus Christ, the Supreme High Priest"; a character is imprinted on bishops "through the imposition of hands and the words of consecration, the grace of the Holy Spirit is so conferred, and the sacred character so imprinted, that bishops in an eminent and visible way take on the functions of Christ the Teacher, Shepherd and Pontiff and act in his person" (n. 21).[37]

When it comes to describing liturgical functions and ministering, *Lumen Gentium* refers generously to the bishop, in particular to his responsibility for preaching and the ministry of the word. It then relates the ministry of bishop to that of priest:

> Christ, whom the Father has sanctified and sent into the world (see Jn 10,36), has through his apostles, made their successors, the bishops, share in his consecration and his mission; and these have legitimately handed on the offices of their ministry in varying degrees to various subjects in the church. In this way the divinely instituted ecclesiastical ministry is exercised in different orders by those who right from ancient times are called bishops, priests [*presbyteri*, "presbyters"] and deacons. Although they do not possess the highest honour of the pontificate and depend on the bishops for the exercise of their power, priests [*presbyteri*, "presbyters"] nevertheless are united with them in priestly honour and by virtue of the sacrament of order, they are consecrated in the image of Christ the one mediator (see 1 Tim 2,5), and proclaim the divine word to all people. But it is above all in the Eucharistic worship or synaxis that they

79

exercise their sacred function, when, acting in the person of Christ and proclaiming his mystery, they unite the prayers of the faithful to the sacrifice of their head, and in the sacrifice of the mass make present and apply, until the coming of the Lord (see 1 Cor 11,26), the one sacrifice of the new testament, that is, the sacrifice of Christ who once and for all offers himself as an unblemished victim to the Father (see Heb 9,11–28). For the faithful who are penitent or who are sick they exercise fully the ministry of reconciliation and comfort, and they convey to God the Father the needs and prayers of the faithful (see Heb 5,1–3). According to their share of authority they exercise the office of Christ the shepherd and head, they gather together the family of God as a fellowship inspired by the spirit of unity and lead them through Christ in the Spirit to God the Father. In the midst of the flock they adore him in spirit and truth (see Jn 4,24). Finally, they labour in preaching and teaching (see 1 Tim 5,17), believing what they have read and meditated in the law of the Lord, teaching what they have believed and putting into practice what they have taught.

As prudent cooperators of the episcopal order and its instrument and help, priests [presbyteri, "presbyters"] are called to serve the people of God and constitute along with their bishop one presbyterium [unum presbyterium] though destined for different duties. In the individual local congregations of the faithful in a certain sense they make the bishop present and they are united with him in a spirit of trust and generosity; and in accordance with their position they undertake his duties and his concern and carry these out with daily dedication. (n. 28)[38]

Under the authority of the bishop, priests sanctify and govern the portion of the Lord's flock entrusted to them, in their own locality they make visible the universal church and they provide powerful help towards the building up of the whole body of Christ (see Eph 4,12). However, attentive always to the welfare of the children of God, they are to take pains that their work contributes to the pastoral work of the whole diocese, and indeed of the whole church. Because of this sharing in the priesthood and mission [*propter hanc in sacerdotio et missione participationem*] priests [*presbyteri*] are to recognize the bishop as truly their father and reverently obey him. The bishop, for his part, is to consider the priests [*sacerdotes*] his cooperators as sons and friends, just as Christ calls his disciples no longer servants but friends (see Jn 15,15). By reason, therefore, of order and ministry, all priests [*omnes sacerdotes*], both diocesan and religious, are associated with the body of bishops and according to their grace and vocation they work for the good of the whole church. (n. 28)[39]

While *Lumen Gentium* makes copious references to the bishops' responsibility of governance, the assertion here that priests share in that governance is notable and deserves fuller theological debate and refinement. Clearly related to this is the often cited *tria munera* of priest, prophet, and king, with "shepherd" regularly replacing "king" in contemporary magisterial literature.[40] Again, this deserves further theological discussion and refinement.

Chief among *Lumen Gentium's* most notable and extremely important assertions is the "universal call to holiness" in chapter 5. "There is one holiness cultivated by all who are led by the Spirit of God" (n. 41). In addressing the church's pastors, it states:

In the first place, the pastors [*pastores*] of Christ's flock in accordance with the pattern set by the eternal high Priest, must carry out their ministry [the Latin contains the precise words *pastoris et episcope*, here translated as "ministry"] with holiness and zeal, with humility and courage. Fulfilled in this way their ministry will be also for themselves an excellent means of sanctification. Called to the fullness of the priesthood [*sacerdotii*], they receive a sacramental grace which enables them perfectly to fulfill their duty of pastoral love through prayer, the offering of the holy sacrifice and preaching and through everything that calls for episcopal care and service. Nor need they be afraid to give their lives for their sheep and, making themselves an example for their flock, they should lead the Church, also by their own example, to a daily higher level of holiness.

Priests [*presbyteri*, "presbyters"] form the spiritual crown of the bishop, and like the order of bishops they share in their grace of office through Christ the unique and eternal Mediator. Through daily performance of their office they should grow in the love of God and of their neighbor, safeguard the body of priestly communion, abound in every spiritual good and give to all a living witness to God, rivaling those priests who down the centuries have left a glorious pattern of holiness often in a form of service that was humble and hidden. Their praise lives on in the Church. For their own people and for the whole people of God they have a duty to pray and offer sacrifice, realizing what they are doing and imitating what they are handling; and far from being held back by their apostolic cares, dangers and tribulations, by these very means they should rise to greater heights of sanctity, nourishing and fostering their action from the rich source of meditation, to the delight of the whole of God's Church. All priests [*omnes presbyteri*, "presbyters"], especially those who because of their particular title of ordination are called diocesan priests [*sacerdotes dioecesani*], should bear in mind how much loyal union and generous cooperation with their bishop contributes to their sanctification.

In the mission and grace of the Supreme Priest, those persons also participate in a particular way who belong to a lower order of the ministry, in the first place deacons. Since they are servants of the mysteries of Christ and of the Church., they must keep themselves from all vice, be pleasing to God and be a source of all good in the sight of people. (n. 41)[41]

Given these sets of assertions, it is clear that the episcopacy receives great emphasis in *Lumen Gentium*, in subsequent documents from the Council, and in the theology, especially of the ordained ministry, that emerged from the Council. This emphasis is reinforced by the Decree on the Pastoral Office of Bishops in the Church (*Christus*

Dominus) itself. That presbyters cooperate with the bishops is clearly asserted in number 11, in which the specific word *presbyter* (*cum cooperation presbyterii*) is used. When describing the responsibility to teach the word of God and to celebrate the eucharistic sacrifice, the term *parish priest* is used (*parochorum, parochi*) (n. 30).[42] Where religious priests are referred to, the term *presbyter* (*in presbyteratus*) is used.

What ultimately became the two conciliar documents on the priesthood and priestly formation (*Presbyterorum Ordinis* and *Optatam Totius*) were, like all the other documents of Vatican II, the topics of debate on the floor of the Council and in written submissions to the committees charged with drafting them.[43] That the title of the document on the priesthood/presbyterate evolved from *De Clericis* (1963) to *De Sacerdotibus* (April 1964) to *De Vita et Ministerio Sacerdotali* (October 1964) to its final (official) title *De Ministerio et Vita Presbyterorum* (commonly known as *Presbyterorum Ordinis*, 1965) is of theological interest and import.[44] One could say that this evolution reflected the mind of the Council itself in moving from the post-Tridentine framing of issues to different approaches, often highly influenced by what is sometimes termed (in an overgeneralized way) a *ressourcement* approach to theology and church life.[45]

OPTATAM TOTIUS AND *PRESBYTERORUM ORDINIS*— DECREE ON PRIESTLY FORMATION (1965) AND DECREE ON THE MINISTRY AND LIFE OF PRIESTS (1965)

Throughout the debates on these texts, it was clear that the vision and assertions of *Lumen Gentium* were to stand as the basis for any particular treatment of the ordained priesthood. In that sense these were understood as intrinsically related to that constitution and, by their nature as "decrees" and not "constitutions," as derivative. Yet, there is also the important reality that some topics "matured" with the debates and subsequent interventions, and that the time between the initial draft and the final text of 1965 allowed a maturation that would have been impossible at an earlier stage.[46] Whereas the initial drafts of the document on priestly formation received a generally warm reception and modifications in the substance of the text were comparatively few,[47] the same could not be said for the document on priestly (presbyteral) life.[48] For example, the *schema* debated in October 1964 was overwhelmingly voted down that same month,[49] which caused the drafters to work diligently to produce a revision distributed to the Council fathers the day before that session ended, November 20, 1964.[50] When the next revision of the *schema* was discussed in October 1965, criticisms were numerous and far-reaching, and more than ten thousand suggestions for changes were submitted.[51] Concerning the other document, true to its title (*Optatam Totius*), the decree on "priestly formation" (*sacerdotali*) uses the word *priest* consistently throughout the document. Not unlike *Lumen Gentium*, this document gives important emphasis to preaching and catechesis (n. 2) and to preparation for "the ministry of the word" (n. 4).[52]

Among the last of the Council documents to be promulgated, the Decree on the Ministry and Life of Presbyters (*Presbyterorum Ordinis*) had been under discussion for two years. Unlike the text on priestly formation, the word *presbyter* is used very generously in this document—which is especially notable in its opening words and as the titles of sections within the text—while *priest* is used very sparingly. One reason adduced for this was that *sacerdos* referred to all three levels of orders (bishop, presbyter, deacon), while *presbyter* referred specifically to those in the second rank.[53] The theological framework already established in other Vatican II documents is sustained here, with the "royal priesthood" clearly asserted (n. 2) and with the ordained called "ministers in the society of the faithful" (n. 2). The collegial nature of the presbyterate is noted in several places (e.g., n. 2). Not surprisingly, when the document refers to the priestly functions at Mass and in penance, it uses "priest" language. The text asserts that through "the sacred power of orders...[they] offer sacrifice and...forgive sins and they perform their priestly office [*sacerdotali officio*] publicly for men in the name of Christ [*pro hominibus nomine Christi*]" (n. 2).[54] The preaching of the word is regarded as the primary duty of bishops and presbyters (*presbyteri*) (n. 4). This is related to the assertions in the Constitution on Divine Revelation (*Dei Verbum*, also published at the last session of the Council) about the need for "all clergy" (*quapropter clericos omnes*) to be engaged in diligent and careful study of the sacred scriptures (n. 25). *Presbyterorum Ordinis* goes on to say that presbyters exercise the office of Christ, Shepherd and Head, and minister "in the name of the bishop [*nomine episcope*]" (n. 6). When describing the ministry and life of presbyters (chapter 3), the decree regularly uses the term *presbyter* and, interestingly, when the document later refers to the ordained as "ministers of holy things," the term *presbyter* is used in connection with the sacrifice of the Mass (n. 14) where sacerdotal language was used before.[55]

The fact that the carefully worded assertions in *Sacrosanctum Concilium*, *Lumen Gentium*, and *Dei Verbum* (as well as in *Gaudium et Spes*) are understood to be the theological foundations of the Council needs to be recalled here, as does the fact that the well-crafted assertions in these texts about the theology of ordained ministry were the subject of serious debate and careful resolution. In comparison, *Presbyterorum Ordinis* is ambivalent on some of the assertions in *Sacrosanctum Concilium*. For example, while *Presbyterorum Ordinis* asserts that the priest acts "in the person of Christ the Head" (n. 2), it does not say that he acts also "in the name of the church."[56] Similarly, the assertions in number 2 about the offering of the sacrifice of the Mass give the impression that what the baptized offer is separate from what the priest offers. The important assertions of *Sacrosanctum Concilium* (n. 48) should be recalled here.[57] While this same paragraph speaks of the universal priesthood of the faithful, it immediately singles out "official ministers" who hold "the sacred power of order." Undoubtedly, a work in progress in the postconciliar church is articulating the relationship between the priesthood of the baptized and the ministerial priesthood. Unfortunately, *Presbyterorum Ordinis* does not assist in this task.[58]

Because of the perceived inner inconsistencies and limitations, *Presbyterorum Ordinis* was not considered a high watermark in articulating a theology of the priesthood. That the topic of ministerial priesthood took up part of the agenda at the 1967, 1971, and 1974 synods of bishops, that priesthood was the topic of Pope John Paul II's Holy Thursday Letters starting from *Dominicae Cenae* in 1980, and that priestly formation was the topic of the synod of bishops in 1990 all indicate the seriousness with which the church's leadership takes the theology, spirituality, and practice of the ordained priesthood. Could it be argued as well that this also indicates the perceived lack of a clear theology of ordained priesthood in the documents of Vatican II?

Among the several things that could be said by way of summary, it is clear that the Second Vatican Council's theology of the ordained priest/presbyter (with both terms generously used) is intrinsically and intimately related to that of the diocesan bishop. It is especially clear in *Lumen Gentium* that the model for the interrelationship of bishop, priest/presbyter, and deacon is derived from the documents of the patristic era.[59] I would argue as well that the role of bishop (*episcopos*) in the patristic era reflected a number of functions that derived from and led to the Eucharist at which he presided and preached the word. These functions included church governance, education, spiritual leadership, and the correction of errors to preserve authentic (orthodox) Catholic teaching.

The clear advantage of underscoring the relationship of bishop to priest/presbyter is the collegiality expressed and presumed in these texts. That Vatican II said little about nondiocesan priests—for example, monk priests, mendicant priests, priests in apostolic societies—has been assessed as a disadvantage. It might also be argued that, precisely because of the influence of the patristic era on this theology, the document could not deal with or sustain a theology of religious and priests in apostolic life simply because they evolved at later periods in the church's life. That the "monk priest" is a phenomenon that defies easy categorization is clear from the way the proscriptions in the *Rule of St. Benedict* have been interpreted and lived.[60]

At the same time, there are a number of challenges inherent in trying to sustain this "patristic" vision in today's world. Among them are the very size of some (arch)dioceses; the increased responsibilities bishops have on a national and international level (such as membership in Vatican congregations, councils, and commissions, and/or the college of cardinals); and the reality that most priests minister in their parish or other pastoral assignments, apart from the bishop whom they see and meet only on occasion. One result of this has been the appointment in some (arch)dioceses of vicars for clergy, as well as the now-customary personnel and assignment boards. These very useful realities have the disadvantage of distancing bishops from priests/presbyters ever further. In addition, an increasing number of diocesan priests appear to function in a way that is more reflective of the medieval church: they serve on their own in parishes and thus live out the attendant medieval theology of ordination that focused on the presbyters' power to consecrate the Eucharist, rather than reflecting the patristic practice and tenet whereby the Eucharist is celebrated by the diocesan bishop with elders, deacons, and so forth, for the local church.

This example raises the whole issue of the relationship between bishop and priest/presbyter. While sociological considerations and the size of most modern dioceses clearly make it impossible to imitate the patristic experience of ordained ministry, are there not additional factors that militate against being able to fulfill the Council's assertions? For example, diocesan bishops can be and are transferred from one diocese to another (at least in the experience of the church in the United States for the past few decades), and it is expected that they will retire at age seventy-five. At the risk of sounding indelicate, might longevity be part of the reason why bishops are transferred? The fact that we live longer than our forebears in the patristic era might have the consequence that people desire a new challenge, or that their accomplishments are notable and they are called to share that leadership in another place. When they were still cardinals, both Joseph Ratzinger and the late Bernard Gantin asserted that a bishop, once appointed to a diocese, should stay there the rest of his life instead of being transferred to a larger see. This would discourage careerism in the episcopate.[61]

A bishop who is not assigned to his home (arch)diocese, or who is transferred to another (arch)diocese, is literally "parachuted in" and asked to make it work. With no prior knowledge of the diocese, he is faced with "on the job training" and has, at the very least, a steep "learning curve." On the other hand, if a bishop is named to his home diocese, might that carry with it the possibility of nepotism and partiality toward one's friends? There is also the issue of auxiliary bishops, ordained for service in a local church. What happens when the diocesan bishop is transferred and a new bishop is named? There are obvious issues of authority at play when a new bishop arrives who may well have a different understanding of the role of auxiliaries and their responsibilities.

Might not the practice of transferring bishops lead to less-personal relatedness to him, with the unfortunate consequence that the bond between bishop and priest presumed in the documents of Vatican II is not the lived experience of many diocesan priests, not to say of priests in monasteries, religious communities, or other societies? Another consequence of the transferal of bishops from one diocese to another is that the college of presbyters within and of the (arch)diocese becomes the de facto source of ministerial stability, without continued reliance on the bishop's leadership and presence. Could one not observe that diocesan presbyters are a source of stability even when they do not surround the bishop who is, theologically and theoretically, the stable center of ministry in the (arch)diocese? While there are dangers to the "congregational" model, in which parishes or other institutions style themselves to be independent of the diocesan bishops and the diocese, at the same time the local parish or institution is where most Catholics are nurtured spiritually and function ministerially.

Another factor that might militate against the way the bishop-centered theology of the ordained priesthood, as emphasized in the documents of Vatican II, functions in the church today is the way the papacy has functioned in the pontificates of John Paul II and Benedict XVI. The Vatican has issued clear assertions about the way national bishops' conferences are to function in relation to the Holy See. For example, John Paul II's *Apostolos Suos* (his *motu proprio* letter, On the Theological and Juridical Nature of Episcopal Conferences, 1998) states that a conference of bishops needs both a unanimous vote and the approval of Rome for any document it wants to publish.[62] In addition, the addresses and homilies given by the pope during regular papal trips outside of Rome calls into question the degree of a bishop's leadership in his own (arch)diocese.[63] That Pope John Paul II issued annual letters to priests on Holy Thursday offers us careful teachings and meditations on ordination (and the Eucharist). But what does that say about the role of the local bishop in nurturing and leading his presbyterate spiritually? (It is worth noting that Pope Benedict XVI did not continue the practice.)

What does this style of papacy imply about the teaching authority and preaching responsibility of the local (arch)bishop whose diocese is visited by the pope? Further, one might also ask what ecclesiology of ministry was operating when Pope Benedict XVI addressed the current divisions within the Austrian clergy in a homily given at Rome at the Holy Thursday Chrism Mass in 2012.[64] Is the use of the papal magisterium as exemplified by Pope Benedict's catechesis on the words of institution requiring that the revised vernacular translation in German read "for many" rather than "for all"[65] really traditional in the Catholic Church? What precedents might this set, if any, and are they desirable given Roman Catholic ecclesiology?

POSTCONCILIAR MAGISTERIUM

Among the many post–Vatican II documents related to the priesthood, I have chosen the following to discuss briefly. Again the issue of the relative weight to be accorded magisterial documents comes to the fore so that our interpretation can be as precise as possible with respect to the genre of the text and the intrinsic merits of its argumentation. *Dominicae Cenae* and *Ecclesia de Eucharistia* are encyclicals—pastoral letters written by the pope for the entire church (although *Dominicae Cenae* is specifically addressed to priests and bishops). Encyclicals "are not used for dogmatic definitions but rather to give counsel or to shed greater light on points of doctrine...."[66] In chapter 1, I noted the assertions of both Pope John Paul II and Pope Benedict XVI on the merits of the *Catechism*. Again, while papal apostolic exhortations have traditionally been ranked after encyclicals and before apostolic letters *motu proprio*, the fact that these postsynodal exhortations are not only signed by the pope but are designed to explain and elaborate on the results of the synods of bishops, and are thus a distillation of the synodical process and an act of representatives of the whole episcopal college, would merit greater weight than an apostolic exhortation signed by the pope without the input of the synod process.[67]

DOMINICAE CENAE (1980) AND THE ANNUAL HOLY THURSDAY LETTERS—POPE JOHN PAUL II

At the beginning of *Dominicae Cenae* Pope John Paul II asserts that his declared intention is not to offer a doctrinal treatise on the Eucharist but to offer a personal witness of faith to the central mystery of the Eucharist with a view to securing, within the college of bishops, a common conviction and awareness of the proper conduct of the liturgy of this mystery.[68] At the risk of oversimplification, allow me to indicate four theses contained in this letter:

1. the inseparable, reciprocal connection between church and Eucharist, which has profound consequences for the correct understanding of the nature of the local church and all pastoral ministry (n. 4);
2. the eucharistic liturgy as source of the Christian ethical life and its missionary task (nn. 5, 6, 7);
3. the relationship of the ministerial priesthood and the common priesthood of the baptized to the Eucharist (nn. 2, 7, 8, 9, 12);
4. the theology and liturgy of the word of God in relation to the Eucharist (nn. 2, 4, 10).[69]

The pope asserts that the Eucharist is "above all a sacrifice" (n. 9, 1). Commentators have observed that the point of departure for his thinking here is the way of speaking and thinking of the Council of Trent and post-Tridentine theology, and not that as inspired by contemporary developments in eucharistic theology.[70] With regard to the specific issue of the role of the baptized and ministerial priesthood in offering the Eucharist, the distinction between the liturgical role of the priest and that of the laity was clearly drawn in *Lumen Gentium* (n. 10). This is paraphrased in *Dominicae Cenae*, in which the pope asserts that since the Mass is a true sacrifice, the celebrant, as minister of this sacrifice, is the authentic priest, performing—in virtue of the specific power of sacred ordination—a true sacrifice that brings creation back to God. Although those who participate in the Eucharist do not confect the sacrifice as he does, they offer with him, by virtue of the common priesthood, their own spiritual sacrifices represented by the bread and wine from the moment of their presentation at the altar. (n. 9)

Edward Kilmartin, among others, will argue that this serves as an introduction to a new line of thought that takes its inspiration from the *General Instruction of the Roman Missal* (*GIRM*), which speaks about the "spiritual value and meaning" of the bread and wine being presented "by the faithful" (n. 73).[71] The *GIRM* also states:

In the celebration of Mass the faithful form a holy people, a people of God's own possession and a royal priesthood, so that they may give thanks to God and to offer the unblemished sacrificial Victim not only by means of the hands of the Priest but also together with him and so that they may learn to offer their very selves.[72]

Many commentators see that here a balance is struck between the liturgical roles of priest and laity and the need to affirm the Augustinian doctrine about the total body of Christ as the subject of the eucharistic offering.

To the precise issue of role differentiation between the baptized and the ordained in the offering of the Eucharist, Pope John Paul II's distinction between "spiritual" and "sacramental" here and in other writings is worth further investigation. Clearly, from as early as the Roman Canon, the church's *lex orandi* has the priest say "*offerimus*" with no other modifier. Theologians such as Hans Urs von Balthasar find this a fruitful avenue of departure for addressing the theology of the Eucharist.[73]

Among other notable assertions in these letters are two that touch on our precise topic. The first is the introduction into contemporary magisterial literature of the notion that the priest is an *alter Christus*. In the 1991 Holy Thursday letter, the pope asserts:

In any event, what is needed everywhere is to pray the Lord of the harvest to send out labourers into his harvest" (Mt 9:38). This is a prayer for vocations and likewise a prayer that each priest will attain ever greater maturity in his vocation: in his life and in his service. This maturity contributes in a special way to an increase of vocations. We simply need to love our priesthood, to give ourselves completely to it, so that the truth about the ministerial priesthood may thus become attractive to others. In the life of each one of us, people should be able to discern the mystery of Christ, the mystery from which originates the reality of the sacerdos as *alter Christus*.[74]

That the documents of Vatican II assiduously avoided this term is clear despite the fact that it had been debated as perhaps a fruitful way to describe the ordained. I regard the work by (now Cardinal) Paul Cordes[75] as a key to understanding this concept at Vatican II and a very important source about these debates and the ultimate preference given by the documents of Vatican II to saying that the priest acts *in persona Christi*.[76] That this has spawned important and fruitful debate about what precisely this means has been extraordinarily helpful.[77]

From among the cautions about the usefulness of returning to the term *alter Christus*, allow me to raise two. First, as attested regularly in the baptismal liturgies of the patristic era (e.g., St. Augustine), after the newly baptized emerges from the baptismal bath, he or she is called "another Christ." This phrase was and is, first of all and primarily, a baptismal reference. Second, in an era of individualism and self-concern one of the contributions of an *in persona Christi capitis* theology is that it places the priest in right relationship with Christ and church and militates against any self-preoccupation or self-importance.

In his Holy Thursday Letter of 2000, the pope asserts the familiar postconciliar triad about priestly ministry:

> Our ministry is not of course limited to celebrating the Eucharist: it is a service which includes the proclamation of the Word, the sanctification of the faithful through the Sacraments, and the leadership of God's People in com-

munion and service. But the Eucharist is the point from which everything else comes forth and to which it all returns. Our priesthood was born in the Upper Room together with the Eucharist. (n. 10)[78]

These three—sacramental celebration, proclamation of the word, and pastoral charity—are reiterated, in more or less the same phrasing, in much postconciliar literature. This clearly is a move away from any cultic preoccupation in the self-understanding of the life and ministry of the priest. Trying to place these three in proper relationship theoretically and in pastoral ministry will always remain a challenge. That they are now almost always seen in relation to each other places liturgy in its proper ecclesiological context.

The challenge may possibly be the result of the fact that presbyters now commonly serve more than one parish population. This means an increase in the demands of sacramental ministry, with the unintended consequence that the pastor has less and less time for the presumed and necessary pastoral care of the flocks he serves. Because priest-pastors need to celebrate sacraments regularly in more than one church or worship center, the time constraints imposed by these sacramental and liturgical demands may prevent the pastor from coming to know his people intimately. (Closely related to this phenomenon is the restructuring underway in many dioceses in which "combining" churches or rearranging them into "mission" churches and parish churches often requires the ordained to function in several places without a reduction in liturgical schedules or liturgical commitments.)[79] The frequent consequence is that other pastoral ministers assume day-to-day care for the parishes alongside and sometimes instead of the priest, whose time legitimately spent in liturgical functioning can distance the focus of his priestly ministry from the pastoral charity presumed in these documents.

CATECHISM OF THE CATHOLIC CHURCH (1992)

It is notable that the treatment of holy orders in the *Catechism* is placed in the context of "the sacraments at the service of communion."[80] Although it summarizes much of the Vatican II documents (contextualized by historical references) and postconciliar texts, it makes some particularly notable assertions. Among them is that "the ministerial priesthood is at the service of the common priesthood" (n. 1547). In reference to the function of representing Christ, Head of the Church, before the assembly of the faithful, the *Catechism* asserts that the ministerial priesthood also acts "in the name of the whole Church when presenting to God the prayer of the Church, and above all when offering the Eucharistic sacrifice" (n. 1552). The paragraph that follows draws out this assertion clearly with emphasis on Christology: it is "the whole Body, *caput et membra*, that prays and offers itself....It is because the ministerial priesthood represents Christ that it can represent the Church" (n. 1553); and earlier in this same paragraph, it says: "in the name of [it does not say "the *person* of"] the whole Church." That there are two degrees of ministerial participation in the priesthood of Christ—episcopacy and presbyterate—is noted. The diaconate "is intended to help and serve them."

It is noteworthy that number 1563 quotes verbatim from *Presbyterorum Ordinis,* number 2. The assertion here that "through the sacrament...priests [*presbyteri*, 'presbyters'] are signed with a special character" is particularly notable because further along, the *Catechism* uses the term *character* in asserting: "Deacons share in Christ's mission and grace in a special way. The sacrament of Holy Orders marks them with an *imprint* ('character') which cannot be removed and which configures them to Christ, who made himself the 'deacon' or servant of all" (n. 1570). As was observed above, the Council of Trent asserted that a character is imprinted at holy orders. It is important to recall that this was preceded by important medieval theological debate about sacramental character and orders, specifically that Bonaventure argued that all (ten) minor and major orders imprint a character because these ordinations are irrepeatable.[81] In addition, Thomas Aquinas's assertions that the sacramental character imprinted at baptism, confirmation, and holy orders orient the recipient to divine worship is an extremely helpful way to underscore their interrelationship.[82] The fact that the liturgy of each of these sacraments employs the use of chrism is important evidence that these sacraments are intrinsically interrelated. It also contextualizes the understanding of holy orders in a dynamic way. With regard to the precise assertion about the deacon marked with "an *imprint* ('character')," it is notable that the footnote reference in the *Catechism* is to the New Testament (Mark 10:45; Luke 22:27) and the patristic era (St. Polycarp's *Letter to the Philadelphians* 5, 2), but not to another ecclesiastical (magisterial) document, especially when one recalls the principle, noted above, that "the individual doctrines that the *Catechism* affirms have no other authority than that which they already possess."[83]

The notion of sacramental character associated with ordination has clearly received some increased attention of late.[84] Such discussions could benefit from the medieval debates (among others) to assure that any tendency toward a personality cult or a cult of the ordained is avoided.[85]

PASTORES DABO VOBIS—POSTSYNODAL EXHORTATION OF POPE JOHN PAUL II (1992)

At the very beginning of this important document, the outcome of the 1990 Synod on Priestly Formation, Pope John Paul II refers to the synodal process and its universal character and also quotes from the bishops' own "Final Message of the Synod to the People of God" (n. 4). This should be borne in mind in interpreting the text, and it should be kept in mind that it reflects an exercise in episcopal and papal teaching. That *Pastores Dabo Vobis* has had direct and important impact on priestly formation is attested to by the way seminaries today regularly refer to the "areas" (sometimes called "pillars") of formation: human (particularly notable in numbers 43 and 44), spiritual, intellectual, and pastoral formation.

While clearly in the trajectory of christological emphasis in the conciliar and postconciliar documents we have addressed, this exhortation does seem to break (welcome) new ground by referring to the Trinity and to the life of the priest "in communion":

"The priest's identity," as the synod fathers wrote, "like every Christian identity, has its source in the Blessed Trinity," which is revealed and is communicated to people in Christ, establishing, in him and through the Spirit, the Church as "the seed and the beginning of the kingdom." The apostolic exhortation *Christifideles Laici*, summarizing the Council's teaching, presents the Church as mystery, communion and mission: "She is mystery because the very life and love of the Father, Son and Holy Spirit are the gift gratuitously offered to all those who are born of water and the Spirit (cf. Jn. 3:5) and called to relive the very communion of God and to manifest it and communicate it in history [mission]."

It is within the Church's mystery, as a mystery of Trinitarian communion in missionary tension, that every Christian identity is revealed, and likewise the specific identity of the priest and his ministry. Indeed, the priest, by virtue of the consecration which he receives in the sacrament of orders, is sent forth by the Father through the mediatorship of Jesus Christ, to whom he is configured in a special way as head and shepherd of his people, in order to live and work by the power of the Holy Spirit in service of the Church and for the salvation of the world.

In this way the fundamentally "relational" dimension of priestly identity can be understood. Through the priesthood which arises from the depths of the ineffable mystery of God, that is, from the love of the Father, the grace of Jesus Christ and the Holy Spirit's gift of unity, the priest sacramentally enters into communion with the bishop and with other priests in order to serve the People of God who are the Church and to draw all mankind to Christ in accordance with the Lord's prayer: "Holy Father, keep them in your name, which you have given me, that they may be one, even as we are one…even as you, Father, are in me, and I in you, that they also may be in us, so that the world may believe that you have sent me" (Jn. 17:11, 21). (n. 12)[86]

This (more theoretical) expression of the trinitarian aspect of priesthood is given a clearer ecclesiological focus and explanation throughout the document, especially in its discussions of relationships (n. 15), the relation of the priesthood to the baptized (n. 17), and pastoral charity (n. 21). In what has come to be expected as postconciliar language it asserts:

> This is the ordinary and proper way which ordained ministers share in the one priesthood of Christ. By the sacramental anointing of holy orders, the Holy Spirit configures them in a new and special way to Jesus Christ the head and shepherd; he forms and strengthens them with his pastoral charity; and he gives them an authoritative role in the Church as servants of the proclamation of the Gospel to every people and of the fullness of Christian life of all the baptized. (n. 15)

Pope John Paul II adds another new dimension to the life of the priest when he refers to the spousal relationship of Christ and the church, and the priest taking the place of Christ. In *Pastores Dabo Vobis* he states:

> Christ's gift of himself to his Church, the fruit of his love, is described in terms of that unique gift of self made by the bridegroom to the bride, as the sacred texts often suggest. Jesus is the true bridegroom who offers to the Church the wine of salvation (cf. Jn. 2:11). He who is "the head of the Church, his body, and is himself its savior" (Eph. 5:23) "loved the Church and gave himself up for her, that he might sanctify her, having cleansed her by the washing of water with the word, that he might present the Church to himself in splendor, without spot or wrinkle or any such thing, that she might be holy and without blemish" (Eph. 5:25–27). The Church is indeed the body in which Christ the head is present and active, but she is also the bride who proceeds like a new Eve from the open side of the redeemer on the cross.
>
> Hence Christ stands "before" the Church and "nourishes and cherishes her" (Eph. 5:29), giving his life for her. The priest is called to be the living image of Jesus Christ, the spouse of the Church. Of course, he will always remain a member of the community as a believer alongside his other brothers and sisters who have been called by the Spirit, but

in virtue of his configuration to Christ, the head and shepherd, the priest stands in this spousal relationship with regard to the community. "Inasmuch as he represents Christ, the head, shepherd and spouse of the Church, the priest is placed not only in the Church but also in the forefront of the Church." In his spiritual life, therefore, he is called to live out Christ's spousal love toward the Church, his bride. Therefore, the priest's life ought to radiate this spousal character, which demands that he be a witness to Christ's spousal love and thus be capable of loving people with a heart which is new, generous and pure—with genuine self-detachment, with full, constant and faithful dedication and at the same time with a kind of "divine jealousy" (cf. 2 Cor. 11:2) and even with a kind of maternal tenderness, capable of bearing "the pangs of birth" until "Christ be formed" in the faithful (cf. Gal. 4:19). (n. 22)

With regard to celibacy specifically, *Pastores Dabo Vobis* asserts:

It is especially important that the priest understand the theological motivation of the Church's law on celibacy. Inasmuch as it is a law, it expresses the Church's will, even before the will of the subject expressed by his readiness. But the will of the Church finds its ultimate motivation in the link between celibacy and sacred ordination, which configures the priest to Jesus Christ the head and spouse of the Church. The Church, as the spouse of Jesus Christ, wishes to be loved by the priest in the total and exclusive manner in which Jesus Christ her head and spouse loved her. Priestly celibacy, then, is the gift of self in and with Christ to his Church and expresses the priest's service to the Church in and with the Lord. (n. 29)

Pope John Paul II's unique theological anthropology is operative here in ways that reflect his theology of the body. That spousal imagery is used in relation to priestly celibacy is evident as early as Pope Paul VI's encyclical *Sacerdotalis Caelibatus*.[87] Spousal imagery was part of the argument in the Declaration on the Admission of Women to Ministerial

Priesthood from the Congregation for the Doctrine of the Faith (1976)[88] and in Pope John Paul II's apostolic letter of 1994, *Ordinatio Sacerdotalis*.[89] Whether or not this spousal imagery is carried through and deepened by contemporary and future theologians and by official church documents remains to be seen. That it has gained some traction in some quarters is clear.[90]

References to the ministry of the priest abound in *Pastores Dabo Vobis*. These include the notable references to abiding in the word of God (n. 26), to liturgy as a "school" for learning how to respond to the call to the priestly vocation" (n. 38), to the importance of *lectio divina* (n. 47), to the ministry of the word (n. 57), and to the Eucharist in the life of the priest (n. 48).[91]

The relationship of the priest to a particular church is addressed and fleshed out with the explicit reference to the legitimate possibilities of "diversities" within the presbyterate (nn. 31–32). My own sense is that these paragraphs can help to flesh out how the college of presbyters functions in dioceses, both in relation to the diocesan bishop and as distinguished from him. Throughout the document the terms *priest* and *presbyterate* are both used. It is particularly notable that *presbyterate* is used when referring to the priest's relationship with others in the presbyterate (n. 23) and to the bishop-priest relationship (n. 31).

ECCLESIA DE EUCHARISTIA—ENCYCLICAL OF JOHN PAUL II (2003)[92]

This encyclical letter of Pope John Paul II reflects the intrinsic relationship between the Eucharist and ecclesiology, so much so that the text has been regarded as being more reflective of the first millennium of the church's life—and of the patristic era in particular—than of the second, although obvious words are used that derive from the medieval debates and practices about the Eucharist in that era as well.

With regard to the ordained priest the document uses familiar language when it states that the priest "puts his voice at the disposal of the One who spoke these words in the Upper Room" (n. 5) and that acting "*in persona Christi* the priest brings about the Eucharistic Sacrifice" and "offers it to God in the name of all the people" (n. 28).

But what is notable is the number of places in which "presbyter" language is used, not "priest." For example:

> This minister is a gift which the assembly *receives through episcopal succession going back to the Apostles*. It is the Bishop who, through the Sacrament of Holy Orders, makes a new presbyter by conferring upon him the power to consecrate the Eucharist. Consequently, "the Eucharistic mystery cannot be celebrated in any community except by an ordained priest, as the Fourth Lateran Council expressly taught." (n. 29; italics in the original)

"Presbyter" language continues when the pope addresses the "sacramental incompleteness" of Sunday worship when priests are not present to celebrate Mass, which "requires the presence of a presbyter, who alone is qualified to offer the Eucharist *in persona Christi*. When a community lacks a priest, attempts are rightly made somehow to remedy the situation so that it can continue its Sunday celebrations" (n. 32).

SACRAMENTUM CARITATIS (2007) AND *VERBUM DOMINI* (2010)—POSTSYNODAL EXHORTATIONS OF POPE BENEDICT XVI

While these documents introduce nothing new about a theology of the ordained priesthood, they make important assertions about the responsibility of the priest/presbyter in the proclamation of the word. *Sacramentum Caritatis* emphasizes the importance of the homily at Mass (n. 46)[93] and *Verbum Domini* makes several statements about the priest's role in enabling the liturgy to be a privileged setting for the word of God (nn. 52ff, with a footnote to the *Lectionary for Mass* Introduction); the "performative character" of the proclaimed word (n. 53); the "sacramentality of the word" (n. 56); the importance of the homily (n. 59); and ending with reference to the assertions of *Pastores Dabo Vobis* about the importance of the liturgy (n. 80).[94]

Chapter Four

Toward a Contemporary Theology of the Ordained Priesthood in Light of the Magisterium

Taking into account my foregoing arguments and my personal observations on the important advances made in the magisterium, as well as observations on some limitations in the contemporary magisterium regarding the ordained priesthood, I will now offer some thoughts about six things that, taken together, might begin to give shape to a contemporary theology of the ordained priesthood in light of the magisterium.

1. BAPTISMAL AND ORDAINED PRIESTHOOD(S)

Lumen Gentium stresses the fundamental equality of all the faithful, established as the new people of God through baptism. In the words of Avery Dulles, "This view serves as a corrective to a traditional understanding of the Church as a *societas inaequalium*...."[1]

Allow me to offer the image of three concentric circles operative here. The largest is the priesthood of Christ, the second within it is the priesthood of the baptized, and the third at the center is the ministerial priesthood. For me this diagram indicates the importance of Christ's high priesthood to ground the others, and the others as related intrinsically to Christ and to each other. Baptism is the foundation and

101

the fundamental ecclesial-identification sacrament. The charisms of all the baptized are charisms and gifts for the upbuilding of the church. Priests minister to and serve all the baptized, from among whom other ministers are delegated and selected. Classic Catholic theology notes that the sacramental distinction between the ordained priesthood and the priesthood of all believers is deep and abiding: a baptized Christian is not what an ordained Christian is called to be and cannot do the things that an ordained Christian is called to do.

As asserted in *Lumen Gentium*, however, the laity are also to be involved in Christ's life and mission:

> [Jesus Christ] associates [the laity] intimately with his life and mission and has also given them a share in his priestly office of offering spiritual worship....For all their works, if done in the Spirit, become spiritual sacrifices acceptable to God through Jesus Christ; their prayers and apostolic works, their married and family life, their daily work, their mental and physical recreation. (n. 34)

But the *Code of Canon Law* omits this specific foundation for the mission of the baptized; for example, canon 225.2 speaks about the lay mission to bring the spirit of the gospel to temporal affairs, but does not refer to the common priesthood. Canon 216 states that all the *christifideles* participate in the church's mission but does not specify the origin of this participation in the *munus* of Jesus Christ, the Priest.[2]

As a sacramental theologian I find it theologically important that, in the rite of presbyteral ordination revised after Vatican II, the bishop consecrates the hands of the ordained with chrism and not with the oil of catechumens, as in the rite used after Trent.[3] That chrism is used at baptism, confirmation or chrismation, and also ordination is of import both liturgically and theologically. Recall the prayer at the anointing with chrism at baptism: "[The] God of power and Father of our Lord Jesus Christ now anoints you with the chrism of salvation, so that united with his people, you may remain forever a member of Christ who is Priest, Prophet and King." Recall that the bishop says the following when he anoints the palms of the hands of the new priests:

The Lord Jesus Christ,
whom the Father anointed with the Holy Spirit and power,
guard and preserve you
that you may sanctify the Christian people
and offer sacrifice to God.

That this translation places the church before offering sacrifice to God is at least ecclesiologically notable.

2. ECCLESIAL LIFE AND ORDAINED MINISTRY IN THE "COMMUNIO" OF THE TRINITY

That Western theologies of ordination to the diaconate, presbyterate, and episcopacy have strong christological emphases is clear, as is the importance of the *in persona Christi capitis* theology at Vatican II and since.[4] At the same time, there is the important theological foundation to be recalled that at baptism we are incorporated into the life of the Trinity as experienced in the church. This trinitarian/ecclesial context needs to be recalled even as the high Christology of orders is respected. That all of the consecratory prayers in the post–Vatican II rites of ordination follow the same pattern expressed in (almost) all other revised blessing and consecratory prayers in the liturgy—that they contain anamneses and epicleses—makes the important theological point that all sacraments take place by asking the Father to send the Spirit to sanctify persons (explicit epiclesis attests to this). While I regard the term *christomonism* as overused, there is a sense in which a christomonistic approach to understanding the priest's identity can be limiting. Issues of exactly how the ordained "represent" Christ and act "in the name of the church" are not always easy to explain theologically. "In the person of Christ" should not be understood as "instead of the person of Christ" or experienced as "in the person of Jesus" (which ordination is not). It is important to underscore that the ordained assume a mystical identification with Christ in order that Christ the Priest may be experienced in the church, and equally or even more important to emphasize that any and all of this depends on the action and abiding presence of the Spirit in the church.

That the Trinity in general and the work of the Holy Spirit in particular are wider than the church and constitute a wider theological category than the ordained helps to contextualize the life and ministry of priests. The presumed *communio* of the Trinity as three equal persons leads to the notion that the ordained—baptized into trinitarian life and ordained in the trinitarian life of the church—abide in the three persons of the one God in their life and mission in the church. Again the theological value of the epiclesis in the prayer texts of almost all of the reformed liturgies after Vatican II lies in its statement that all that we do and are is done by invoking and abiding in the Trinity.

At least since the Extraordinary Synod of 1985 about Vatican II, the term *communio* has sustained several meanings and has been widely and well used to describe a number of realities in the life of the church. Pope John Paul II, we must remember, explicitly links the obligations and rights of the faithful with their participation in the threefold office of Christ.[5] It has been argued that *communio* is behind the assertions in canon law that "baptism is the act by which an individual is incorporated into Christ, made a member of the People of God, and given participation in the three fold *munera* of Christ, priest, prophet and king" (204.1). An obvious related issue is, What is particular to the ordained vis-à-vis the lay faithful?[6]

My own sense is that a "both…and" rhetoric is important here to try to place in relationship ways of describing *communio* between the baptized and the ordained. The baptized and the ordained priesthoods should be understood to be in a dynamic, mutually respectful, and enriching relationship that builds up the body of Christ so that the ecclesiology of communion lies at the root of all levels on which the church exists: *communio fidelium, ecclesiarum et ministrorum.* Clearly, canons 208 to 23 provide the infrastructure of communion[7] and presume earnest efforts by the bishop to insure and sustain communion among the laity and his priests and deacons.[8]

One important theological advantage in using the term *communio* is that it relies on the communion of persons that is the Blessed Trinity and the church that is incorporated into them.[9] *Communion* as a real symbol of God's grace necessarily implies the presence of the Holy Spirit. "Thus, given that *communio* has its ultimate foundation in the intratrinitarian life, participation in which is communicated through the Church of Christ (and especially baptism), the Holy Spirit's presence is constitutive of the reality which *communion* symbolizes."[10]

3. STEWARDS OF THE TRADITION

The contemporary magisterium has clearly spelled out that preaching is an essential part of the life of the priest. That part of the priest's life is to be a teacher is stressed in several documents and, indeed, is exemplified in the papacies of John Paul II and Benedict XVI. The preaching/teaching role requires in-depth study of the scriptures and of the Catholic magisterial and intellectual tradition. The role of the Jewish rabbi forms a major part of the background here; from it we derive not (just) "knowledge" but also the notion of abiding in God through word and theology. The privilege of handing on to others what we have received is as foundational as St. Paul's admonitions in 1 Corinthians 11 and 15. Abiding in and being a man of *tradition* is the absolute foundation for this role of being a faithful steward of the word. But I would like to draw this out a bit further by asserting that the priest is responsible for articulating our tradition in ways that always respond to the questions raised by contemporary cultures and philosophies. The diocesan priest especially must be immersed in things of the holy just as he is immersed in the things of this earth and the here and now. In that sense the priest is faithful to the Catholic theological tradition, which always needs to be a dialogue partner in developing modes of expression. If we merely repeat the familiar concepts of former ages, we are not faithful to the church's perennial challenge and privilege to give voice to the word in ever new ways and circumstances and within the variety of cultures that is Catholicism.

I find the distinction between *traditio* and *tradita* helpful. By *traditio* I mean the incredible wealth of what we have received from over two thousand years of meditating on, proclaiming, and preaching the word of God on the basis of our theological tradition. By *tradita* I mean the specific application of *traditio* at a given place and time. Part of the ongoing ministry of the priest is to create new ways of articulating who and what we are for the contemporary world. It is always new *tradita* based on the abiding *traditio* that is Catholicism. The deposit of faith is not a lockbox, unable to be opened and sorted out in new ways. Rather, it is unfolded in an ongoing, sustained, rigorous, and professional commitment to theology and church practice.

The admonition to the deacon at his ordination to "believe what you read, teach what you believe, and practice what you teach" rings true for all of the ordained—bishop and presbyter included. That preaching has been a hallmark of the liturgical reform is clear, as is the fact that it needs a firm foundation and ongoing engagement in prayer, study, writing, and witness to these truths in everyday life. The ordained is clearly charged with this responsibility. Might it be an impediment to priestly ordination if one cannot preach or teach well?

4. MEMBER OF A COLLEGE OF PRESBYTERS

The magisterial documents we have reviewed emphasize the ecclesial and collegial character of the ordained priest. The ordination rite whereby one is ordained "to the presbyteral order" specifies that the diocesan priest is a member of the diocesan college of presbyters. The documents of Vatican II were primarily concerned with the diocesan priesthood, something that has been a cause of some critique. Yet, the importance of other "kinds" of priests cannot be denied, among whom are monks, mendicants, missionaries, other kinds of religious, and priests from societies, institutes, and new ecclesial movements.[11] This is to suggest that there is a fundamentally communitarian notion of the priestly vocation in a diocese with a variety of kinds of priests (diocesan, monks, mendicants, apostolic societies and institutes, and so forth), all related in understandably different degrees to the diocesan bishop.

At the same time, some of the possible strains in the presbyter/bishop relationship noted above in light of *Lumen Gentium's* assertions should be recalled here. In effect, most priest-pastors live more of a medieval model, as parish priests celebrating sacraments in a parish, than a patristic model whereby bishop and presbyter are in direct relationship and presumably regular contact.

In addition to working with the diocesan presbyteral council, many diocesan bishops take important initiatives to gather presbyterates regularly for study days, retreats, and convocations. But still these are held on occasion, and regular contact between bishop and priest is often not possible.

It is notable that *Pastores Dabo Vobis* also indicated strains within presbyterates. Certainly some recent sociological studies of American presbyters offer real data about this; they also employ such terms as "veterans of the campaign," "Vatican II priests," "Pope John Paul II and Benedict XVI priests," and so on.[12]

In fact, we should also be priests of the Pope Leos: Leo the Great in the fifth century, who gave us a rich theology of the incarnation; and Leo XIII in the late nineteenth and early twentieth centuries, who published *Rerum Novarum* and encouraged academic study and theological inquiry.

We should be priests of the Gregorys: Gregory the Great in the late sixth and early seventh centuries and Gregory VII in the eleventh, each of whom served at a time of significant and much needed reform in church life.

We should be priests of the Piuses: Pius X in the earliest years of the twentieth century, who brought us (among other things) liturgical participation and early and frequent communion; and Pius XII in the mid-twentieth century, who offered us landmark encyclicals on sacred scripture, the liturgy, and the (then called) mystical body of Christ.

We should be priests of John XXIII, pastoral visionary and astute church leader, who convoked and presided at the first sessions of the Second Vatican Council.

We should be priests of Paul VI, who continued Vatican II and insisted on traveling to learn from and preach to the world church.

We should (all) be priests of John Paul II, who combined both names of his predecessors and was for us the indeed far more peripatetic pope, who loved philosophy and taught us a philosophical approach to many things.

We should (all) be priests of Benedict XVI, whose theological training and clarity of teaching heartens all of us in realizing that theology is a Catholic strong suit against fundamentalists who utter proof texts rather than study and revere texts to be probed, understood, and assimilated.

We should (all) be priests of Francis, whose mission and apostolate consciousness reflect his Jesuit background and whose choice of name has been repeatedly backed up by concern for the world's poor in charity and in inviting reflection on economic structures that impoverish many for the benefit of the few.

Popes are "servants of the servants of God." They are also called *pontifex*—literally, "bridge builders"—who inspire us to build bridges among local churches with fellow presbyters as companions on the journey. That bishops serve in the same "bridge-building" capacity should also be evident. One of the bridges that need to be continually rebuilt is within and among presbyters.[13]

Given the mobility of bishops and the fact that many retire from office rather than die in office, the diocesan presbyterate necessarily bears some of the responsibility for unity and leadership (governance as well?) that traditionally resides with the bishop. Priests already know and experience this. Collegial structures of collaboration with the diocesan bishop assist this.

5. PRESIDER AT LITURGICAL PRAYER

With the post–Vatican II liturgical reform, the term *preside* has gained increased emphasis in liturgical books. The *General Instruction of the Roman Missal* uses the terms *preside*, *presidential*, and *presiding* no fewer than fifteen times: for example, it states that the priest exercises "his office of presiding over the gathered assembly" (n. 31) and that "the nature of the 'presidential' parts requires that they be spoken in a loud and clear voice and that everyone listen to them attentively" (n. 32). From as early as the second century, St. Justin the Martyr referred to the one who "presided" at the liturgy to distinguish him from the reader, deacon, and so forth. The fact that certain prayers of the liturgy are designated as "presidential prayers" follows that tradition. The specific presidential prayers are the Eucharistic Prayer, the Opening Prayer, the Prayer over the Gifts, and the Prayer after Communion. The term refers to the priest's precise role at these parts of the Mass as speaking in the name of Christ and the church but in such a way that these actions do not diminish the role of the whole assembly in celebrating the liturgy. At the same time the *GIRM* sanctions our use of the term *celebrant*. It refers to the *celebrant* of the Mass (priest or bishop) twice as many times as it uses *presider* (and if you add the term *concelebrant*, that number grows significantly). My sense is that when the word *preside* or a variation is used, it refers to the particular liturgical functions to be fulfilled by the ordained. *Celebrant*, on the other hand, most often refers to the person of the priest or bishop himself as he functions in the liturgy. That the term *preside* delineates one role is clear; that it also presumes the functioning of other ministers is equally clear. The president is not the only focal point in the liturgy. He is the office-bearer of the community, before whom he is responsible.

From an ecclesiological perspective, the term *presider* presumes the relatedness of the presiding priest's relationship with the community (recalling that *sacerdos* originally referred to the diocesan bishop, then to presbyters as well). The thesis that one presides because one is in a leadership position is clear.[14] While understanding and appreciating the role of the mendicant and the missionary, there is an important principle and rule of thumb to be sustained here, namely, the interrelationship of preaching the word, presiding at liturgy, and pastoral care. The triad made popular in the recent magisterium is as traditional as the *Apology* of Justin the Martyr and the patristic era from which so much insight in the contemporary magisterium is gleaned. It is a triad that marks much postconciliar writing on the ordained priesthood.

6. ENDURING PRESENCE *IN* AND *FOR* THE CHURCH

The sacramentality of orders is based on symbol systems that under-score how a sacrament is a sign—a visible thing, an action, or a person that reveals something invisible through something material and that achieves a spiritual goal such as building up the church. With regard to ordained ministry, a major aspect of the symbol systems involved is the church. I believe that the stale debates about "state" or "function" can be transcended by appreciating the symbol systems that are operative in and through the ministry of the person of the ordained priest in the church.

In addition, I judge that any (proper) emphasis on the ministries performed by the priest must be set in dynamic relationship with the minister's personal witness. At the same time I want to avoid a theology of ministry that is a personality cult of the ordained. My own sense of the debates about *in persona Christi*, in which the conventional understand-ing of the individual priest and his powers as nuanced at Vatican II and since, is that it is about personal (and communal) self-transcendence. Ordained priests minister as much in imitation of St. John the Baptist ("I am not the Messiah"), as they do in the person of Christ (not himself) in the name of the church (including himself) in relationship to others.

In a world of impermanence and transience,[15] the import of perma-nent witness on behalf of the church cannot be gainsaid. This raises the issue about terms of office for pastors (for example, it is often six years, renewable for another six) and for parochial vicars (normally shorter), and whether they add to instability in terms of church belonging and church participation. In terms of sociological research about vocations, it has been established that when pastors stay for longer periods of time than terms of office, the number of vocations in a parish rises.

Not unrelated to this, in my estimation, is the need for enduring symbols of hope in a fractured world. More often than we care to admit, I will argue, a collective loss of hope and hopefulness is present in some parts of church life today. That priests can be and are enduring symbols of hope is highly desirable, not to say admirable. Emmanuel is always with us, often (obviously) incarnated in and through human beings.

Notes

INTRODUCTION

1. See Francis A. Sullivan, *Creative Fidelity: Weighing and Interpreting Documents of the Magisterium* (Eugene, OR: Wipf and Stock, 2003); original, Paulist Press, 1996, 1.

2. For a useful contemporary overview of the complex topic of the various meanings of *magisterium* and the relative authority of magisterial documents, see Avery Dulles, *Magisterium: Teacher and Guardian of the Faith* (Naples: Sapientia Press, 2007), much of which expands on his "Lehramt und Unfehlbarkeit," in Walter Kern, Josef Pottmeyer, and Max Seckler, eds., *Handbuch der Fundementaltheologie 4: Traktat Theologische Erkenntnislehre* (Fribourg: Herder, 1988), 153–78.

3. The literature on this issue is vast. See Pope Benedict XVI's address to the Roman Curia, December 22, 2005, (http://www.vatican.va/holy_father/benedict_xvi/speeches/2005/december/documents/hf_ben_xvi_spe_20051222_roman-curia_en.html). This will be discussed below in the section on "interpreting Vatican II on the priesthood."

4. See *Sacramenta: Bibliographia Internationalis* (Rome: Pontifical Gregorian University Press, 1992), vol. 1, xvi.

5. See Francis G. Morrisey, *The Canonical Significance of Papal and Curial Pronouncements* (Washington, DC: Canon Law Society of America, 1978), 21–22. Also see Sullivan, *Creative Fidelity*.

6. See Sullivan, *Creative Fidelity*, 21, and author's personal correspondence with Drs. Patrick Granfield and Paul J. McPartlan.

7. For example, the insightful if very brief piece by Richard Gaillardetz, "Conversation Starters, Dialogue and Deliberation at Vatican II," *America* (February 13, 2012).

8. The literature on reception is vast, complex, and enormously important. Among other sources that I regard as "classic," see Angel

Anton, "La 'reception' en la Iglesia y ecclesiologia," *Gregorianum* 77, no. 1 (1996): 57–96; and "La 'reception,' II," *Gregorianum* 77, no. 3 (1996): 437–69; Alois Grillmeier, "Konzil und Rezeption," *Theologie und Philosophie* 45 (1970): 321–52; Salvatore Vitiello, "Ricezione," in *Dizionario di Ecclesiologia*, ed. Gianfranco Calabrese, Philip Goyret, Orazio Francesco Piazza (Firenze: Città Nuova, 2010, revised ed.), 1198–202; Thomas Rausch, "Reception," in *New Dictionary of Theology*, ed. Dermot Lane, Mary Collins, Joseph Komonchak (Collegeville, MN: Liturgical Press, 1989), 828–31; Yves Congar, "La 'Reception' comme réalité ecclésiologique," *Revue des Sciences Philosophiques et Théologiques* 56 (1972): 369–403; William C. Rusch, "'Baptism, Eucharist and Ministry'—and Reception," *Dialog* 22 (1983): 85–93.

9. See http://www.vatican.va/holy_father/benedict_xvi/speeches/2005/december/documents/hf_ben_xvi_spe_20051222_roman-curia_en.html.

10. Giuseppe Alberigo, ed., *The History of Vatican II*, 5 vol., English edition ed. Joseph A. Komonchak (Leuven: Peeters / Maryknoll, NY: Orbis Books, 1995–2006).

11. Herbert Vorgrimler, ed., *Commentary on the Documents of Vatican II* (New York: Herder and Herder, 1967–69); original German, *Zweite Vatikanische Konzil. Dokumente und Kommentar.*

12. For example, the stellar essay by Joseph A. Komonchak, "Toward an Ecclesiology of Communion," in *The History of Vatican II*, vol. 4, 1–94.

13. Giuseppe Alberigo, *A Brief History of Vatican II*, trans. Matthew Sherry (Maryknoll, NY: Orbis Books, 2006). This is a condensed version of the Conclusions from all five volumes.

14. Agostino Marchetto, *Il concilio ecumenico Vaticano II: Contrappunto per la storia* (Roma: Libreria Editrice Vaticana, 2005); *The Second Vatican Ecumenical Council: A Counterpoint for the History of the Council*, trans. Kenneth D. Whitehead (Scranton, PA: University of Scranton Press, 2010).

15. The fact that the subtitle is *Una storia mai scritta* ("The Story Never Written") is somewhat telling. The text itself is filled with unfamiliar insights, many of which, in my judgment, do not correspond to the facts, and many of which reflect superficial knowledge of them (Turin: Lindau, 2010).

16. Massimo Faggioli, *Vatican II: The Battle for Meaning* (New York/Mahwah, NJ: Paulist Press, 2012).

17. Faggioli, *True Reform: Liturgy and Ecclesiology in Sacrosanctum Concilium* (Collegeville, MN: Liturgical Press, 2012).

18. Ormond Rush, *Still Interpreting Vatican II: Some Hermeneutical Principles* (New York/Mahwah, NJ: Paulist Press, 2004).

19. Richard Gaillardetz, *The Church in the Making: Lumen Gentium, Christus Dominus, Orientalium Ecclesiarum* (New York/Mahwah, NJ: Paulist Press, 2006).

20. John W. O'Malley, *What Happened at Vatican II* (Cambridge, MA: Belknap Press of the Harvard University Press, 2008). While this insightful book has received generally favorable reviews and has been translated into foreign languages, among the most critical reviews is that of John McDermott, "Did That Really Happen at Vatican II?" *Nova et Vetera* 8, no. 2 (2010): 425–67.

21. John O'Malley, "'The Hermeneutic of Reform': A Historical Analysis," *Theological Studies* 73 (September 2012): 517–46.

22. For example, the Latin text of *Sacrosanctum Concilium* is found at http://www.vatican.va/archive/hist_councils/ii_vatican_council/documents/vat-ii_const_19631204_sacrosanctum-concilium_lt.html.

23. That there is a significant debate underway about how to interpret the documents of Vatican II is clear. Among a host of other sources, see Alberigo's *History of Vatican II* and his *A Brief History of Vatican II*. Also see Vorgrimler, *Commentary on the Documents of Vatican II*; Marchetto, *Il concilio ecumenico Vaticano II;*; Roberto De Mattei, *Il concilio Vaticano II: Una storia mai scritta* (Torino: Lindau, 2010); O'Malley, *What Happened at Vatican II*; and Faggioli, *Vatican II: The Battle for Meaning*.

CHAPTER ONE

1. Despite the fact that John Paul II's *Spiritus et Sponsa* (December 4, 2003) on the fortieth anniversary of the promulgation of *Sacrosanctum Concilium* also fits into this time frame, it is about liturgy in general and is rather hortatory in style; therefore, it will not be discussed.

2. As far as possible, Mass translations will be from texts from the Vatican Web site.

3. In addition, it is important to note that issues surrounding the Eucharist at Trent also concerned what priestly ordination meant and the role of the ordained at Mass. See, among others, David N. Power, *The Sacrifice We Offer: The Tridentine Dogma and Its Interpretation* (New York: Crossroad, 1987), which skillfully uses the *acta* of Trent as well as assertions made by those who participated in it (bishops, heads of religious communities, theologians). Similarly today, what became known as the "Holy Thursday Letters" of Pope John Paul II on the priesthood deserve study and reflection for what they say about the Eucharist. See Pope John Paul II, *Letters to My Brother Priests: Complete Collection of Holy Thursday Letters (1979–2005)* (Woodbridge, IL: Midwest Theological Forum, 2006), and, among others, the trenchant commentary on the first letter by Edward J. Kilmartin, *Church, Eucharist, and Priesthood* (New York/Mahwah, NJ: Paulist Press, 1981).

4. Among others, see Piet Fransen, "Sacraments, Signs of Faith," in *Hermeneutics of the Councils*, collected by H. E. Mertens and F. De Graeve (Leuven: University Press, 1985), originally published in *Worship* 37 (1962): 31–50. Another (parallel) fruitful avenue for research not pursued here (because of its breadth and scope) would be to summarize and assess the way the Eucharist is viewed and described in the contents of the prayers, other texts, and rites of the *Missale Romanum* published after Trent, and of the *Missale Romanum* published after Vatican II and its subsequent versions (1970, 2002, and 2009). The results gleaned would further the contemporary interest in the relationship of the church's *lex orandi* to its *lex credendi*, some of which is summarized in my own *Models of the Eucharist* (New York/Mahwah, NJ: Paulist Press, 2005), the method of which is largely derived from my own *Context and Text: Method in Liturgical Theology* (Collegeville, MN: Liturgical Press, 1994), 44–81. For a summary of other contemporary European and American approaches to "liturgical theology," see my own *Liturgical Theology: A Primer*, American Essays in Liturgy (Collegeville, MN: Liturgical Press, 1990). Among the more important current authors dealing with liturgical theology is Joris Geldghof, "Liturgy as Theological Norm: Getting Acquainted with Liturgical Theology," *Neue Zeitschrift fur systematische Theologie und Religionsphilosophie* 52 (2010): 155–76.

5. Among other issues that are important to note: the relationship of the emperor to the bishops and other church leaders—that is, the matter of church and state, or the "politics" of the Trent's deliberations; the authoritative response of the Catholic Church to reformers like Luther and Calvin; the move toward a standardization of the Order of Mass in the Roman Rite; and the need for addressing the two central issues of controversy about the Eucharist—(real) presence and sacrifice—as well as the role of the ordained priest at Mass.

6. For a more complete discussion of these premises, see my own *Models of the Eucharist.*

7. See, for example, the assertion of Paul VI in *Mysterium Fidei*, n. 24:

> And so the rule of language which the Church has established through the long labor of centuries, with the help of the Holy Spirit, and which she has confirmed with the authority of the Councils, and which has more than once been the watchword and banner of orthodox faith, is to be religiously preserved, and no one may presume to change it at his own pleasure or under the pretext of new knowledge. Who would ever tolerate that the dogmatic formulas used by the ecumenical councils for the mysteries of the Holy Trinity and the Incarnation be judged as no longer appropriate for men of our times, and let others be rashly substituted for them? In the same way, it cannot be tolerated that any individual should on his own authority take something away from the formulas which were used by the Council of Trent to propose the Eucharistic Mystery for our belief. These formulas—like the others that the Church used to propose the dogmas of faith—express concepts that are not tied to a certain specific form of human culture, or to a certain level of scientific progress, or to one or another theological school. Instead they set forth what the human mind grasps of reality through necessary and universal experience and what it expresses in apt and exact words, whether it be in ordinary or more refined language. For this reason, these formulas are adapted to all men of all times and all places.

Translation from http://www.vatican.va/holy_father/paul_vi/encycli cals/documents/hf_p-vi_enc_03091965_myster ium_en.html.

8. Among others are the following references in the Tridentine decrees on the Eucharist (notably its sacrificial nature): "On the Manner of Living and Other Points to Be Observed by the Council" (Session 2); "Decree on Justification" (Session 6); "The True and Catholic Doctrine of the Sacrament of Order, to Condemn the Errors of Our Time" (Session 23); "Decree on Reform," canon 1 (Session 23); "Decree on Purgatory" (Session 25). These can be found in Norman Tanner, ed., *Decrees of the Ecumenical Councils*, vol. 2 (Washington, DC: Georgetown University Press, 1990), 693–737.

9. Avery Dulles explains these "statements of condemnation:
> The term "anathema" in the Hebrew Scriptures often refers to a curse, setting a person or thing apart for destruction. In 1 Cor. 16:22 and Gal. 1:8–9, St. Paul used the word to denote separation from the Christian community or excommunication. In the early councils the term was regularly used in condemnation of heresy, a practice that still continued as late as Vatican I. The 1917 Code of Canon Law treats anathematization as a solemn excommunication (c. 2257, 2). The Code of 1983, however, makes no reference to anathemas.

From *Magisterium: Teacher and Guardian of the Faith* (Naples: Sapientia Press, 2007), 62–63, fn. 5.

10. Ibid., 68. See fn. 9 where Dulles asserts: "On the authority of the chapters and canons at the Council of Trent and Vatican I, see Ioachim Salaverri, *De Ecclesia Christi in Sacrae Theologiae Summa*, vol. 1: *Theologiae Fundamentalis*, Part III, nos. 906–13, pp. 811–16."

11. Tanner, *Decrees of the Ecumenical Councils*, 693–98.

12. Ibid., Decree on the Most Holy Sacrament of the Eucharist, n. 1.3, p. 694.

13. Ibid, 5.24, p. 695.

14. Ibid., canon 1, p. 695; canon 3, p. 697.

15. Ibid., 697–98.

16. Among others, see the very important study by Alexander Gerken, *Theologie der Eucharistie* (Munich: Kosel, 1973).

17. All quotations in this paragraph are from Tanner, *Decrees of the Ecumenical Councils*, 693–97.

18. The footnote reference given for these assertions is from St. Augustine, *De Civitate Dei* 10.5. However, the Latin word used in the

chapter is *symbolum*, not *signum*, which word was used by Augustine. Here the Tanner translation should read *symbol*, not *sign*.

19. Whereas the title used here is *Doctrina et Canones*, the title for the section on the holy sacrament is *Decretum*.

20. Tanner, *Decrees of the Ecumenical Councils*, 735.

21. That this latter decree reiterates the value of the Mass as "daily offered by priests on the altar" and is a "sacrifice" is noteworthy as these reiterate the major assertions of the canons on the sacrifice of the Mass.

22. Tanner, *Decrees of the Ecumenical Councils*, 732–33.

23. Ibid., 733.

24. Ibid.

25. Ibid.

26. Ibid.

27. Ibid., 735. This is an important statement since it asserts that the celebration of sacraments in the vernacular is possible. The same is reiterated in *Sacrosanctum Concilium*, nn. 36 and 63. Some argue that because Vatican II does not mandate the vernacular that liturgy should not be so celebrated. Such an assertion flies in the face of precisely what *Sacrosanctum Concilium* asserts and the role of national episcopal conferences in relation to the Holy See in granting such permission. My own sense is that a detailed study of the literature from 1965 through 1971 (or so), outlining the decisions made about the vernacular, would be a very worthwhile contribution given the polemics surrounding this issue today.

28. Tanner, *Decrees of the Ecumenical Councils*, 736.

29. It is notable that this decree asserts that "the very life-giving victim by whom all have been reconciled to God the Father is daily offered by priests on the altar [*in altari per sacerdotii quotidian immolator*]," Tanner, *Decrees of the Ecumenical Councils*, 736. What is of interest is the emphasis placed on both "immolation" and the "propitiatory" value of the Mass in subsequent catechetical and magisterial literature. See, for example, the commentaries accompanying the hand missals: *Nouveau Paroissien Romain* (Paris: H. Mignard, 1905), 78–91, and *Messalino Festive e Vesperale* (Padova: Il Messagero di S. Antonio, 1959), 29–37, where "immolation" is equated with "consecration," and where "communion" is equated with "consummation of the victim."

30. Dulles, *Magisterium*, 70. The possibility of "dissent" from the Roman Catholic ordinary magisterium as put forth in a papal encyclical has been one of the more neuralgic issues facing post-1968 Catholicism, the year that *Humanae Vitae* was published. Among the best treatments in English of what the post-Tridentine manuals of theology say about the possibility of dissent, see Joseph A. Komonchak, "Ordinary Papal Magisterium and Religious Assent," in Charles Curran, ed., *Contraception: Authority and Dissent* (New York: Herder and Herder, 1968, and reprinted in Curran's *Readings in Moral Theology*, vol. 3, New York/Mahwah, NJ: Paulist Press, 1982), 67–90.

31. All quotations from *Mediator Dei* are from http://www.vatican.va/holy_father/pius_xii/encyclicals/documents/hf_p-xii_enc_20111947_mediator-dei_en.html.

32. It is at least noteworthy that the use of "my sacrifice and yours" in this context is used in a positive way to underscore the laity's involvement. However, the newly revised English language translation of *meum ac vestrum sacrificium* from the former ICEL (International Commission on English in the Liturgy) rendering "our sacrifice" to "my sacrifice and yours" has caused no little negative reaction. It is also to be noted that this text itself is controverted in that its origins are debated and original meanings also debated. That it might become an assertion of the role of the ordained over against the assembly and their role in offering the Eucharist would be regrettable. See my own "Which Liturgy is the Church's Liturgy?" *Origins* 38, no. 37 (February 26, 2009): 581–89, and more recently, "Mediated Immediacy: Sacramentality and Textual Multivalence in the Catholic Liturgy," the Hovda Lecture, delivered July 18, 2011, National Association for Pastoral Musicians, online posting in process.

33. Pope John Paul II asserts that the priest offers the sacrifice *sacramentally* and the laity offer it *spiritually*. A particularly completing exposition of the fundamental ecclesiological understanding of the Eucharist through an exploration of *offerimus* is in the chapter "The Mass, a Sacrifice of the Church?" in Hans Urs Von Balthasar's *Explorations in Theology*, vol. 3, *Creator Spirit* (San Francisco: Ignatius Press, 1993), 185–243. This issue also comes up in the documents of Vatican II; see below in both the text and notes.

34. Number 27 of *Mediator Dei* reads:

This efficacy, where there is question of the eucharistic sacrifice and the sacraments, derives first of all and principally from the act itself (*ex opere operato*). But if one considers the part which the Immaculate Spouse of Jesus Christ takes in the action, embellishing the sacrifice and sacraments with prayer and sacred ceremonies, or if one refers to the 'sacramentals' and the other rites instituted by the hierarchy of the Church, then its effectiveness is due rather to the action of the Church (*ex opere operantis Ecclesiae*), inasmuch as she is holy and acts always in closest union with her Head.

35. Number 44 of *Mediator Dei* states: "Since, therefore, it is the priest chiefly who performs the sacred liturgy in the name of the Church, its organization, regulation and details cannot but be subject to Church authority. This conclusion, based on the nature of Christian worship itself, is further confirmed by the testimony of history."

36. All quotations from *Sacrosanctum Concilium* are from http://www.vatican.va/archive/hist_councils/ii_vatican_council/docu ments/vat-ii_const_19631204_sacrosanctum-concilium_en.html.

37. Among others, see Burkhard Naunheuser, "Der Beitrag der Liturgie zur theologischen Erneuerung," *Gregorianum* 59 (1969): 589–614. The phrase itself, *opus nostrae redemptionis exercetur*, is found in the Prayer over the Gifts on the Second Sunday *per annum* and at the Evening Mass of the Lord's Supper in the present (post–Vatican II) *Missale Romanum*; it was in the *Secreta* on the Ninth Sunday after Pentecost in the former (post-Trent) Missal.

38. See the important detailed study of the drafting of this part of the Constitution on the Sacred Liturgy in Michael Witczak, "The Manifold Presence of Christ in the Liturgy," *Theological Studies* 59 (1998): 680–702.

39. See Council of Trent, Session 22, Doctrine on the Holy Sacrifice of the Mass, c. 2, Tanner, *Decrees of the Ecumenical Councils*, 733–34.

40. Pope Pius X, "*Motu Proprio* on Sacred Music," *Tra le sollecitudini* (1903).

41. The literature on this topic is vast and not all of it is without bias, especially in favor of the former Missal and in limiting some of the familiar ways that participation is customarily engaged in today. Among many others, see Frederick R. McManus, *Liturgical Participation: An Ongoing Assessment* (Collegeville, MN: Liturgical Press, 1988); *Actuosa Participatio. Conoscere, comprendere e vivere la Liturgia.* Studi in

onore del Prof. Domenico Sartore, a cura di Agostino Montan, Manlio Sodi (Citta del Vaticano: Libreria Editrice Vaticana, 2002); and R. Gabriel Pivarnik, *Toward a Theology of Liturgical Participation* (Collegeville, MN: Liturgical Press, 2013) 1–52.

42. Among others, see the very valuable work of Maurizio Barba, *La reforma conciliare dell' "Ordo Missae." Il percorso storico-redazionale del riti d'ingresso, di offertorio e di comunione.* Nuova edizione (Roma: Edizioni Lliturgiche, 2008), and *L'Institutio Generalis del Missale Romanum. Analysi storico-redazionale dei riti d'ingresso, di offertorio e di comunione* (Roma: Libreria Editrice Vaticana, 2005).

43. This is not to suggest that some recent initiatives concerning the authorized celebration of the "extraordinary form" of the Eucharist in the Roman Rite (the Tridentine Mass) has not been the cause of some fierce debates and assertions about the theological and liturgical value of the post–Vatican II Missal, often called the "Missal of Paul VI," and now called the "Missal of Pope John Paul II" because it was revised during his pontificate. (The post-Tridentine Missal is now called the "Missal of Blessed John XXIII" because the 1962 edition of that Missal is the one now sanctioned for limited use.)

44. All quotations from *Mysterium Fidei* are taken from http://www.vatican.va/holy_father/paul_vi/encyclicals/documents/hf_p-vi_enc_03091965_mysterium_en.html.

45. For a helpful overview of these terms see Edward Schillebeeckx, *The Eucharist*, trans. N. D. Smith (New York: Sheed and Ward, 1968), 9–21 and 87–160. See also his article "Transubstantiation, Transfinalization, Transignification," in *Living Bread, Saving Cup: Readings on the Eucharist*, ed. R. Kevin Seasoltz (Collegeville, MN: Liturgical Press, 1982), 175–89.

46. See note 7 of this chapter for the text from *Mysterium Fidei* n. 24.

47. Under the subhead "Greater Clarity of Expression Always Possible," *Mysterium Fidei* immediately goes on to say in n. 25:

> They [the formulas] can, it is true, be made clearer and more obvious; and doing this is of great benefit. But it must always be done in such a way that they retain the meaning in which they have been used, so that with the advance of an understanding of the faith, the truth of faith will remain unchanged. For it is the teaching of the First Vatican Council that "the

meaning that Holy Mother the Church has once declared, is to be retained forever, and no pretext of deeper understanding ever justifies any deviation from that meaning."

48. The text of Trent is faithfully reproduced in the Latin: illud in primis, quod huius doctrinae est veluti summa et caput, iuvat meminisse, scilicet per Mysterium Eucharisticum Sacrificium Crucis, semel in Calvaria peractum, admirabili modo repraesentari, iugiter in memoriam revocari eiusque virtutem salutarem in remissionem eorum quae quotidie a nobis committuntur peccatorum applicari (cf. CONCIL. TRID., *Doctrina de SS. Missae Sacrificio*, c. 1). Unfortunately the Latin *repraesentari* is rendered "re-enacted" in the Vatican online English translation of *Mysterium Fidei*, n. 27, which term is not the same as "re-presented."

49. The apostolic constitution *Fidei Depositum* is itself contained in the *Catechism of the Catholic Church* (Washington, DC: United States Catholic Conference, 1994), 5.

50. Francis A. Sullivan, *Creative Fidelity: Weighing and Interpreting Documents of the Magisterium* (Eugene, OR: Wipf and Stock, 2003), 12, 17.

51. With regard to the genre of the *Catechism of the Catholic Church*, the General Directory for Catechesis from the Congregation for Clergy (1997) states:

n. 124. It is important to understand the literary genre of the *Catechism of the Catholic Church* in order to foster the role which the Church's authority gives to it in the exercise and renewal of catechetical activity in our time. The principal characteristics of this follow:

—The *Catechism of the Catholic Church* is above all a catechism; that is to say, an official text of the Church's Magisterium, which authoritatively gathers in a precise form and in an organic synthesis the events and fundamental salvific truths which express the faith common to the People of God and which constitute the indispensable basic reference for catechesis.

—In virtue of being a catechism, the *Catechism of the Catholic Church* collects all that is fundamental and common to the Christian life without "presenting as doctrines of the faith special interpretations which are only private opinions or the views of some theological school."

—The *Catechism of the Catholic Church* is, moreover, a catechism of a universal nature and is offered to the entire Church. It presents an updated synthesis of the faith which incorporates the doctrine of the Second Vatican Council as well as the religious and moral concerns of our times. However, "by design this Catechism does not set out to provide the adaptation of doctrinal presentations and the catechetical methods required by the differences of culture, age, spiritual maturity and social and ecclesial condition amongst all those to whom it is addressed. Such indispensable adaptations are the responsibility of particular catechisms and, even more, of those who instruct the faithful" (n. 434).

See http://www.vatican.va/roman_curia/congregations/cclergy/documents/rc_con_ccatheduc_doc_17041998_directory-for-catechesis_en.html.

52. Among others, see John A. Renken, "The Personal Ordinariate for Former Anglicans in the United States," *Worship* 86, no. 3 (May 2012): 208–22.

53. See *Catechism of the Catholic Church* (Washington, DC: United States Catholic Conference, 1994), nn. 1076–1205. Subsequent citations from nn. 1210–1405 are from this translation of the *Catechism*.

54. Ibid., nn. 1210–1321. That the term *sacraments of initiation* is used here and in the Rite of Christian Initiation of Adults is itself noteworthy since this phrase was coined only in the latter part of the nineteenth century. See Pierre-M. Gy, "La notion chrétienne d'initiation," *La Maison-Dieu* 132 (1977): 39–44.

55. Pope John Paul II devoted several weekly audience addresses to the Eucharist. See the following weekly English editions of *L'Osservatore Romano*: "Eucharist is a Celebration of Divine Glory," no. 40 (October 4, 2001), p. 11; "Eucharist: 'Memorial' of God's Mighty Works," no. 41 (October 11, 2001), p. 11; "Eucharist is a Perfect Sacrifice of Praise," no. 42 (October 18, 2001), p. 11; "Eucharist, Banquet of Communion with God," no. 43 (October 25, 2001), p. 11; "The Eucharist, 'a Taste of Eternity in Time,'" no. 44 (November 1, 2001), p. 11; "Eucharist is a Sacrament of the Church's Unity," no. 46 (November 15, 2001), p. 11;

"Word, Eucharist and Divided Christians," no. 47 (November 22, 2001), p. 11.

56. While the genre of such "letters" is legitimately debated, the fact that *Ecclesia de Eucharistia* is called an "encyclical" means that it has the same teaching authority as other encyclicals treated herein.

57. All quotations in this section from *Ecclesia de Eucharistia* are from http://www.vatican.va/holy_father/special_features/encyclicals/documents/hf_jp-ii_enc_20030417_ecclesia_eucharistia_en.html. All italics in the quotations are in the original.

58. See Norman Tanner, "The Eucharist in the Ecumenical Councils," Gregorianum 82, no. 1 (2000): 37–49 at 38.

59. The pope incorrectly asserts in n. 2 that the paschal Triduum is from Holy Thursday evening through Easter Sunday morning. In fact, it ends with second Vespers on Easter Sunday (see *General Norms for the Liturgical Year*, n. 19).

60. That he uses the texts of the *Novus Ordo Missae* here is significant because the Mass used after Trent stated "this is my body" whereas the revised post–Vatican II Mass states "this is my body given for you."

61. The theme of stewardship in order to share what we currently have is taken up again in Pope Benedict XVI's encyclical *Deus Caritas Est*, n. 20:

> Love of neighbour, grounded in the love of God, is first and foremost a responsibility for each individual member of the faithful, but it is also a responsibility for the entire ecclesial community at every level: from the local community to the particular Church and to the Church universal in its entirety. As a community, the Church must practise love. Love thus needs to be organized if it is to be an ordered service to the community. The awareness of this responsibility has had a constitutive relevance in the Church from the beginning: "All who believed were together and had all things in common; and they sold their possessions and goods and distributed them to all, as any had need" (*Acts* 2:44–5). In these words, Saint Luke provides a kind of definition of the Church, whose constitutive elements include fidelity to the "teaching of the Apostles", "communion" (*koinonia*), "the breaking of the bread" and "prayer" (cf. *Acts* 2:42). The element of "communion" (*koinonia*) is not initially defined, but appears con-

cretely in the verses quoted above: it consists in the fact that believers hold all things in common and that among them, there is no longer any distinction between rich and poor (cf. also *Acts* 4:32–37). As the Church grew, this radical form of material communion could not in fact be preserved. But its essential core remained: within the community of believers there can never be room for a poverty that denies anyone what is needed for a dignified life.

See http://www.vatican.va/holy_father/benedict_xvi/encyclicals/docu ments/hf_ben-xvi_enc_20051225_deus-caritas- est_en.html.

62. The preference for "presbyter" language in other documents of Vatican II, as opposed to "priest" language, is evident in the conciliar Decree on the Ministry and Life of Presbyters (*Presbyterorum Ordinis*), despite the fact that many English-language translations use the word *priests* to translate what should read *presbyters*.

63. Among the more important commentaries on traditional usages of *in persona Christi* and *in persona ecclesiae*, see Bernard-Dominique Marliangeas, *Clés poue une Theologie du Ministere* (Paris: Editions Beauchesne, 1978). For what is regarded as the classic commentary on the Vatican II document on the priestly life (*Presbyterorum Ordinis*), see Paul Josef Cordes, *Sendung zum Dienst. Exegetisch-historische und systematische Studien zum Konsilsdekret "Von Dienst und Leben der Priester"* (Frankfurt am Main: Josef Knecht, 1972).

64. More on these issues throughout the text and notes for chapter 3.

65. See John Paul II's apostolic letter *Dies Domini*, written about five years earlier: http://www.vatican.va/holy_father/john_paul_ii/ apost_ letters/documents/hf_jp-ii_apl_05071998_dies-domini_ en.html.

66. See *Sunday Celebrations in the Absence of a Priest*, rev. ed. (Chicago: Liturgy Training Publications, 2012; original, United States Conference of Catholic Bishops, 1992). This is the American title for rituals to be used when the Sunday Eucharist cannot be celebrated. The Canadian title is *Sunday Celebration of the Word and Hours* (Ontario: Canadian Conference of Catholic Bishops, 1995).

67. See John Huels' timely and substantive article "Assessing the Weight of Documents on the Liturgy," *Worship* 74 (2000): 117–35.

68. All quotations from *Redemptionis Sacramentum* come from http://www.vatican.va/roman_curia/congregations/ccdds/documents/ rc_con_ccdds_doc_20040423_redemptionis-sacramentum_en.html.

69. Under this category of "grave matters" are a range of practices, such as the use of unauthorized Eucharistic prayers, the omission of the pope's and local bishop's names in the Eucharistic prayer, no self-intinction, the pouring of consecrated wine from large vessels into smaller chalices, and so on. This latter practice was very common in the United States, and this requirement has caused major adjustments in the manner in which communion under two species is distributed (where it continues to be shared in this way).

70. There is a growing body of literature that deals with relating the actual celebration of the liturgy to the way liturgical theologians understand the *lex orandi, lex credendi* equation. Some like myself call this the *lex agendi*, while others prefer to use *lex agendi* to refer to the way what the liturgy enacts is reflected in life. See my own *Context and Text,* chapter 2, esp. 52–75.

71. The English translation is at http://www.vatican.va/holy_father/ john_paul_ii/apost_letters/documents/hf_jp-ii_apl_20041008_mane-nobiscum-domine_en.html. All italics are in the originals.

72. My own preference is for *lex vivendi.* Again see *Context and Text,* chapter 8, 311–51.

73. Dulles, 55. See, among others, Jozef Tomko, *Sinodo del Vescovi: Natura, Metodo, Prospettive* (Vatican City: Libreria Editrice Vaticana, 1985); Francois Dupre la Tour, *Le Synode des Eveques et la Collegialite* (Malesherbes: Parole et Silence, 2004); as well as Avery Dulles himself, "Synod of Bishops," in *The New Dictionary of Catholic Social Thought,* ed. Judith Dwyer, 930–32 (Collegeville, MN: Liturgical Press, 1994).

74. For the Synod on the Eucharist, they were *Communicato: XI Assemblea Generale Ordinaria del Sinodo dei Vescovi—Publicazione del Linamenta,* May 28, 2004. The *instrumentum laboris* was published on July 7, 2005. It was commonly held that the *lineamenta* was seriously deficient (see, among others, Patrick Reagan, "Quenching the Spirit: The Epiclesis in Recent Roman Documents," *Worship* 79, no. 5 (September 2005): 386–404, at 398–402.

75. "Elenco finale delle Propozioni," in *Synodus Episcoporum Bollettino,* XI Assemblea Generale Ordinaria del Synodo dei Vescovi (2–23 ottobre 2005), at http://www.vatican.va/news_services/press/ sinodo/documents/bollettino_21_xi-ordinaria-2005/bollettino_ 21_xi_ordinaria-2005_index_it.html.

76. All quotations from *Sacramentum Caritatis* are taken from http://www.vatican.va/holy_father/benedict_xvi/apost_exhortations/do cuments/hf_ben-xvi_exh_20070222_sacramentum-caritatis_en.html.

77. Within part 3, "A Mystery to Be Lived," are these considerations of "proclaiming" the mystery:

The Eucharist and mission

84. In my homily at the eucharistic celebration solemnly inaugurating my Petrine ministry, I said that "there is nothing more beautiful than to be surprised by the Gospel, by the encounter with Christ. There is nothing more beautiful than to know him and to speak to others of our friendship with him." These words are all the more significant if we think of the mystery of the Eucharist. The love that we celebrate in the sacrament is not something we can keep to ourselves. By its very nature it demands to be shared with all. What the world needs is God's love; it needs to encounter Christ and to believe in him. The Eucharist is thus the source and summit not only of the Church's life, but also of her mission: "an authentically eucharistic Church is a missionary Church." We too must be able to tell our brothers and sisters with conviction: "That which we have seen and heard we proclaim also to you, so that you may have fellowship with us" (*1 Jn* 1:3). Truly, nothing is more beautiful than to know Christ and to make him known to others. The institution of the Eucharist, for that matter, anticipates the very heart of Jesus' mission: he is the one sent by the Father for the redemption of the world (cf. *Jn* 3:16–17; *Rom* 8:32). At the Last Supper, Jesus entrusts to his disciples the sacrament which makes present his self-sacrifice for the salvation of us all, in obedience to the Father's will. We cannot approach the eucharistic table without being drawn into the mission which, beginning in the very heart of God, is meant to reach all people. Missionary outreach is thus an essential part of the eucharistic form of the Christian life.

The Eucharist and witness

85. The first and fundamental mission that we receive from the sacred mysteries we celebrate is that of bearing witness by our lives. The wonder we experience at the gift God has made to us in Christ gives new impulse to our lives and com-

mits us to becoming witnesses of his love. We become witnesses when, through our actions, words and way of being, Another makes himself present. Witness could be described as the means by which the truth of God's love comes to men and women in history, inviting them to accept freely this radical newness. Through witness, God lays himself open, one might say, to the risk of human freedom. Jesus himself is the faithful and true witness (cf. *Rev* 1:5; 3:14), the one who came to testify to the truth (cf. *Jn* 18:37). Here I would like to reflect on a notion dear to the early Christians, which also speaks eloquently to us today: namely, witness even to the offering of one's own life, to the point of martyrdom. Throughout the history of the Church, this has always been seen as the culmination of the new spiritual worship: "Offer your bodies" (*Rom* 12:1). One thinks, for example, of the account of the martyrdom of Saint Polycarp of Smyrna, a disciple of Saint John: the entire drama is described as a liturgy, with the martyr himself becoming Eucharist. We might also recall the eucharistic imagery with which Saint Ignatius of Antioch describes his own imminent martyrdom: he sees himself as "God's wheat" and desires to become in martyrdom "Christ's pure bread" [citing Ignatius of Antioch]. The Christian who offers his life in martyrdom enters into full communion with the Pasch of Jesus Christ and thus becomes Eucharist with him. Today, too, the Church does not lack martyrs who offer the supreme witness to God's love. Even if the test of martyrdom is not asked of us, we know that worship pleasing to God demands that we should be inwardly prepared for it. Such worship culminates in the joyful and convincing testimony of a consistent Christian life, wherever the Lord calls us to be his witnesses.

78. Number 92 of *Sacramentaum Caritatis* goes on to say:
With these words, the rite not only includes in our offering to God all human efforts and activity, but also leads us to see the world as God's creation, which brings forth everything we need for our sustenance. The world is not something indifferent, raw material to be utilized simply as we see fit. Rather, it is part of God's good plan, in which all of us are called to

be sons and daughters in the one Son of God, Jesus Christ (cf. *Eph* 1:4–12). The justified concern about threats to the environment present in so many parts of the world is reinforced by Christian hope, which commits us to working responsibly for the protection of creation. The relationship between the Eucharist and the cosmos helps us to see the unity of God's plan and to grasp the profound relationship between creation and the "new creation" inaugurated in the resurrection of Christ, the new Adam. Even now we take part in that new creation by virtue of our Baptism (cf. *Col* 2:12ff.). Our Christian life, nourished by the Eucharist, gives us a glimpse of that new world—new heavens and a new earth— where the new Jerusalem comes down from heaven, from God, "prepared as a bride adorned for her husband" (*Rev* 21:2).

79. See my own "Which Liturgy is the Church's Liturgy?" 581–89.

80. For example, *Pastores Dabo Vobis* (1992) following the Synod on the Priesthood (1990), or *Christifidelis Laici* (1988) on the laity following the 1987 synod on that topic.

81. See http://www.vatican.va/holy_father/benedict_xvi/letters/2007/documents/hf_ben-xvi_let_20070707_lettera-vescovi_en.html.

82. See *NewsLetter,* Committee on the Liturgy, vol. 43 (June–July 2007), 20.

83. See Congregation for Divine Worship, *Quattuor Abhinc Annos,* October 3, 1984, and Pope John Paul II, *Ecclesia Dei,* July 2, 1988, which letter document established the Pontifical Commission *Ecclesia Dei.*

84. Hence the inclusion of this *motu proprio* and "letter" in this treatment of recent Roman documents on the liturgy as seen from a theological point of view. The issue in these documents is not what they say about the Eucharist. Rather, it is what they say about church unity and how unity within Catholicism is reflected in the celebration of different liturgies that come from different historical, cultural, and theological contexts.

85. There are a number of issues that these documents have raised, among which is whether the Tridentine Mass was ever really suppressed. See Pope Paul VI's apostolic constitution *Missale Romanum,* approving the new Roman Missal, April 3, 1969:

No one should think, however, that this revision [*renovatio*] of the Roman Missal has come out of nowhere. The progress in liturgical studies during the last four centuries has certainly prepared the way. Just after the Council of Trent, the study "of ancient manuscripts in the Vatican library and elsewhere" as St. Pius V attests in the Apostolic Constitution *Quo primum* helped greatly in the correction of the Roman Missal. Since then, however, other ancient sources have been discovered and published and liturgical formularies of the Eastern Church have been studied....

When he promulgated the *editio princips* of the Roman Missal, our predecessor St. Pius V offered it to the people of Christ as the instrument of liturgical unity and the expression of a pure and reverent worship in the Church. Even though, in virtue of the decree of the Second Vatican Council, we have accepted into the new Roman Missal lawful variations and adaptations, our own expectation in no way differs from that of our predecessor. It is that the faithful will receive the new Missal as a help toward witnessing and strengthening their unity with one another....

We decree that these laws and prescriptions be firm and effective now and in the future, notwithstanding, to the extent necessary, the apostolic constitutions and ordinances issued by our predecessors and other prescriptions, even those deserving particular mention and amendment.

The *Conferentiarum Episcopalium*, October 28, 1974, *Notitiae* 10 (1974): 353, in *Documents on the Liturgy 1963–1979: Conciliar, Papal and Conciliar Texts* (Collegeville, MN: Liturgical Press, 1982) 1784) states:

As to the rules issued by this Congregation in favor of priests who because of their advanced years or infirmity find serious difficulties in using the new Order of Mass in the Roman Missal or the *Lectionary for Mass*, it is clear that an Ordinary has the power to grant them permission to use, in whole or in part, the *Missale Romanum* in the *edition typica* of 1962, as emended by the decrees of 1965 and 1967, but *only* for a celebration *without a congregation*. Ordinaries cannot grant this permission for the celebration of Mass with a congregation. Both local and religious Ordinaries must rather see to it…that all priests and people of the Roman Rite duly accept the Order of Mass in the Roman Missal; that through greater study and reverence they come to appreciate it for the treasures of both the word of God and of liturgical and pastoral teaching this it contains.

If it was not suppressed, there would be no need for such a permission ("indult").

86. English edition of *L'Osservatore Romano*, October 22, 1984.

87. The translation of *Ecclesia Dei* is at http://www.vatican.va/holy_father/john_paul_ii/motu_proprio/documents/hf_jp-ii_motu-proprio_02071988_ecclesia-dei_en.html.

88. "Letter of Pope Benedict XVI accompanying the Apostolic Letter *Summorum Pontificum*," in *Newsletter*, Committee on the Liturgy, vol. 43 (June–July 2007), 21.

89. Ibid.

90. See http://www.vatican.va/holy_father/benedict_xvi/apost_exhortations/documents/hf_ben-xvi_exh_20100930_verbum-domini_en.html.

91. He cites his own *Sacramentum Caritatis*, n. 69, here.

92. On the importance of the homily, the pope asserts in n. 59:
Generic and abstract homilies which obscure the directness of God's word should be avoided, as well as useless digressions which risk drawing greater attention to the preacher than to the heart of the gospel message. The faithful should be able to perceive clearly that the preacher has a compelling desire to present Christ, who must stand at the centre of every homily. For this reason preachers need to be in close and constant contact with the sacred text; they should prepare for the homily by meditation and prayer, so as to preach with conviction and passion.

CHAPTER TWO

1. For a more expansive treatment of a contemporary theology of the Eucharist in light of the evolution of the church's liturgical practice, magisterium, and theology, see my own *Models of the Eucharist* (New York/Mahwah, NJ: Paulist Press, 2005). Both in that book and in this

chapter, I offer ideas that, taken together, may help to draw out a theology of a sacrament that by its nature is all encompassing and impossible to describe or delineate adequately.

2. I am indebted to Edward Kilmartin for this phrase, which appears in several of his writings, including *Church, Eucharist, and Priesthood.*

3. That these acclamations are placed *before* the memorial section of the Eucharistic Prayers has been legitimately debated among scholars. That the acclamations come *after* the memorial sections of the Eucharistic Prayers for children offer an alternative placement. In addition, the fact that these acclamations address Christ in the middle of a prayer that is addressed to the Father has also been the source of some debate among liturgical scholars who argue that the entire prayer is addressed to the Father and, as such, the acclamations are something of an intrusion.

4. Again I am indebted to Edward Kilmartin for originating this phrase.

5. Among others, see the still very useful book by Josef Jungmann, *Christian Prayer Through the Centuries* (New York/Mahwah, NJ: Paulist Press, 2009).

6. See http://www.vatican.va/archive/hist_councils/ii_vatican_council/documents/vat-ii_const_19641121_lumen-gentium_en.html.

7. The comprehensive study by Archdale King, *Eucharistic Reservation in the Western Church* (New York: Sheed and Ward, 1965), is worth serious study for the combination of historical, cultural, and architectural factors that bear on this issue. The principle that reservation for communion to the sick led to adoration was found useful, among others, by the participants in the American Lutheran and Roman Catholic dialogue on the subject of the Eucharist as sacrifice. See *Lutherans and Catholics in Dialogue I, II, III* (Washington, DC: NCCB, 1967).

8. The present *GIRM* is detailed in its description of the tabernacle, stating:

> 314. In accordance with the structure of each church and legitimate local customs, the Most Blessed Sacrament should be reserved in a tabernacle in a part of the church that is truly noble, prominent, readily visible, beautifully decorated, and suitable for prayer.

The one tabernacle should be immovable, be made of solid and inviolable material that is not transparent, and be locked in such a way that the danger of profanation is prevented to the greatest extent possible. Moreover, it is appropriate that, before it is put into liturgical use, it be blessed according to the rite described in the Roman Ritual.

315. It is more in keeping with the meaning of the sign that the tabernacle in which the Most Holy Eucharist is reserved not be on an altar on which Mass is celebrated. Consequently, it is preferable that the tabernacle be located, according to the judgment of the diocesan Bishop—

—either in the sanctuary, apart from the altar of celebration, in a form and place more appropriate, not excluding on an old altar no longer used for celebration (cf. no. 303);

—or even in some chapel suitable for the faithful's private adoration and prayer and organically connected to the church and readily visible to the Christian faithful.

316. In accordance with traditional custom, near the tabernacle a special lamp, fueled by oil or wax, should be kept alight to indicate and honor the presence of Christ.

That the previous GIRM stated a preference for a separate chapel for reservation is clear and was the reason why the previous rubrics in the *Sacramentary for Mass* did not indicate any gestures of reverence to be given to the tabernacle before or after the celebration of the Mass.

9. Probably the best treatment of this is in Nathan Mitchell's *Cult and Controversy: The Worship of the Eucharist Outside of Mass* (New York: Pueblo Publishing Co., 1982).

10. Published in various editions including, for the United States, *Sunday Celebrations in the Absence of a Priest*, rev. ed. (Chicago: Liturgy Training Publications, 2012; original, United States Conference of Catholic Bishops, 1992).

11. For the rite of distributing communion on weekdays outside Mass, see *Holy Communion and Worship of the Eucharist Outside Mass* (Totowa, NJ: Catholic Book Publishing Co., 1991; original, United States Conference of Catholic Bishops, 1976).

12. See "Toward A Ferial Order of Mass," (reprinted in) Anscar J. Chupungco, *Worship: Beyond Inculturation* (Washington, DC: The Pastoral Press, 1994), 107–28.

13. See http://www.catholicherald.co.uk/news/2012/09/14/lay-people-to-preside-at-funerals-in-liverpool/.

14. Among other articles, see "Why I would allow my loved ones a lay-led funeral," *The Tablet*, http://www.thetablet.co.uk/blogs/358/17.

15. James McCartin, *Prayers of the Faithful: The Shifting Spiritual Life of American Catholics* (Cambridge, MA: Harvard University Press, 2010).

16. See John Paul II, *Ecclesia de Eucharistia*, n. 32, http://www.vat ican.va/holy_father/john_paul_ii/encyclicals/documents/hf_jp-ii _enc_20030417_eccl-de-euch_en.html.

CHAPTER THREE

1. See Chapter 1, note 3.

2. All citations from the Council of Trent in Latin and English are from Norman Tanner, ed., *Trent to Vatican II*, vol. 2, *Decrees of the Ecumenical Councils* (Washington, DC: Georgetown University Press, 1990). As will be seen, there are times when the translation needs to be adjusted when the English term *priest* is used to translate both the Latin *sacerdos* and *presbyter*.

3. Ibid., 684.

4. See Piet Fransen, "Sacraments, Signs of Faith," in *Hermeneutics of the Councils*, ed. H. E. Mertens and F. De Graeve (Leuven: University Press, 1985), at 418–19.

5. Tanner, ed., *Decrees of the Ecumenical Councils*, 669.

6. Ibid.

7. Ibid.

8. Ibid., 669–70.

9. Ibid., 685.

10. Ibid., 704 and 707.

11. Ibid., 712.

12. Ibid., 710.

13. Ibid., 711.

14. Ibid., 713.

15. Ibid., 733.

16. Ibid., 735.

17. Ibid.

18. Ibid., 742.

19. Ibid.

20. Ibid.

21. Ibid., 743.

22. Ibid., 744.

23. Ibid., 747.

24. Ibid., 748.

25. Ibid., 749.

26. Ibid.

27. See Nicholas Haring, "St. Augustine's Use of the Word *Character*," *Medieval Studies* 14 (1952): 79–97.

28. Among others, see Alexandre Ganoczy, "'Splendors and Miseries' of the Tridentine Doctrine of Ministries," in Bas van Iersel and Roland Murphy, eds., *Office and Ministry in the Church* (*Concilium* 80; New York: Herder & Herder, 1972), 75–86; and Hervé-Marie Legrand, "The 'Indelible' Character and the Theology of Ministry," in Hans Küng and Walter Kasper, eds., *The Plurality of Ministries* (*Concilium* 74; New York: Herder & Herder, 1972), 54–62.

29. Again see, among others, Francis A. Sullivan, *Creative Fidelity: Weighing and Interpreting Documents of the Magisterium* (Eugene, OR: Wipf and Stock, 2003).

30. Because my focus is more precisely on the theology of ordained priesthood, for astute observations about the decree on priestly formation see Mathijs Lamberights, "*Optatam Totius*. The Decree on Priestly Formation. A Short Survey of Its History at the Second Vatican Council," *Louvain Studies* 30 (2005): 25–48.

31. Tanner, *Decrees of the Ecumenical Councils*, 822.

32. Ibid.

33. Avery Dulles, *The Priestly Life: A Theological Reflection* (New York/Mahwah, NJ: Paulist Press, 1997), 11.

34. Tanner, *Decrees of the Ecumenical Councils*, 857. See *Mediator Dei*, n. 92:

> In this most important subject it is necessary, in order to avoid giving rise to a dangerous error, that we define the exact meaning of the word "offer." The unbloody immolation at the words of consecration, when Christ is made present upon the altar in the state of a victim, is performed by the priest and by him alone, as the representative of Christ and

not as the representative of the faithful. But it is because the priest places the divine victim upon the altar that he offers it to God the Father as an oblation for the glory of the Blessed Trinity and for the good of the whole Church. Now the faithful participate in the oblation, understood in this limited sense, after their own fashion and in a twofold manner, namely, because they not only offer the sacrifice by the hands of the priest, but also, to a certain extent, in union with him. It is by reason of this participation that the offering made by the people is also included in liturgical worship.

See http://www.vatican.va/holy_father/pius_xii/encyclicals/documents/hf_p-xii_enc_20111947_mediator-dei_en.html.

35. Tanner, *Decrees of the Ecumenical Councils*, 857.

36. Ibid., 864.

37. Ibid., 865. The footnote reference here is to the teaching of Trent on character; see Denzinger-Schönmetzer 980.

38. Ibid., 872–73.

39. Ibid.

40. It was John Calvin who coined the phrase *priest, prophet, and king*. References to Christ himself as possessing this threefold ministry preceded its application to the ranks of the ordained.

41. Tanner, *Decrees of the Ecumenical Councils*, 882.

42. Ibid., 924.

43. For summaries of the progression of drafts see, among others, Jan Grootaers, "The Drama Continues Between the Acts: The 'Second Preparation' and Its Opponents," in Giuseppe Alberigo and Joseph Komonchak, *The History of Vatican II*, vol. 2 (Leuven: Peeters, 1997), 483–85, where the author treats these texts under the heading "latecomers." Also Evangelista Vilanova, "The Intersession (1963–64)," in *The History of Vatican II*, vol. 3 (Leuven: Peeters, 2000), 395–98; Norman Tanner, "The Church and the World," in *The History of Vatican II*, vol. 4 (Leuven: Peeters, 2003), 356–64; and Peter Hunnermann, "The Final Weeks of the Council," *The History of Vatican II*, vol. 5 (Leuven: Peeters, 2006), 363–484.

44. In a similar call to be attentive to language, I mentioned earlier in chapter 1 that the parallel wording of the two recent synod titles—Synod on the Eucharist in the Life and Mission of the Church and

Synod on the Word of God in the Life and Mission of the Church—should not be ignored.

45. See, among others, the impressive collection of essays edited by Gabriel Flynn and Paul D. Murray, *Ressourcement: A Movement for Renewal in Twentieth-Century Catholic Theology* (Oxford/New York: Oxford University Press, 2012).

46. Grootaers, "The Drama Continues," 484.

47. Tanner, "The Church and the World," 356–64.

48. Ibid., 346–56.

49. Ibid., 355. The Council fathers voted 930 in favor of the *schema*, 1199 against, which by comparison with any other schema at the Council was a large number. See the "sub secreto" documents: *Schemata Decreti, De Clericis* (Vatican: Typis Polyglottis Vaticanis, 1963); *Schema Propositionum, De Sacerdotibus* (Vatican: Typis Polyglottis Vaticanis, 1964); *Relatio Super Schema Emendatum Propositionum De Sacerdotibus Quod Nunc Inscribitur De Vita et Ministerio Sacerdotali* (Vatican: Typis Polyglottis Vaticanis, 1964); *Schema Decreti, De Presbyterorum Ministerio et Vita. Textus Recognitus et Modi* (Vatican: Typis Polyglottis Vaticanis, 1965). For a brief but very useful compilation of the various *schemata* for the Decree on Priestly Life, see René Wasselynck, *Les Prêtres. Élaboration du Décret Presbyterorum Ordinis de Vatican II. Synopse* (Paris: Desclée, 1968).

50. Ibid., 355.

51. P. Hunnermann, "The Final Workings of the Council," 457.

52. Tanner, *Decrees of the Ecumenical Councils*, 950.

53. Ibid., 346.

54. Ibid., 1043.

55. Ibid., 1044.

56. See Samuel Aquila, "The Teaching of Vatican II on '*In Persona Christi*' and '*In Nomine Ecclesiae*' in Relation to the Ministerial Priesthood in Light of the Historical Development of the Formulae" (licentiate thesis, Collegio Sant'Anselmo, Rome, 1990).

57. Ibid., 18–26.

58. Among others, see Remi Parent, *A Church of the Baptized: Overcoming the Tension between the Clergy and the Laity*, trans. Stephen Arndt (New York/Mahwah, NJ: Paulist Press, 1989); and the more recent (and excellent) work by Jean-Pierre Torrell, *Un peuple sacerdotal*, published in English as *A Priestly People: Baptismal Priesthood and*

Priestly Ministry, trans. Peter Heinegg (New York/Mahwah, NJ: Paulist Press, 2013).

59. See the copious patristic references in nn. 26–33 of *Lumen Gentium*.

60. See my own "On Monastic Priesthood," *American Benedictine Review* 41, no. 3 (September 1990): 225–62.

61. See http://www.catholicnews.com/data/stories/cns/0802630.htm.

62. The English translation of *Apostolos Suos* can be found at http://www.vatican.va/holy_father/john_paul_ii/motu_proprio/docu ments/hf_jp-ii_motu-proprio_22071998_apostolos-suos_en.html.

63. At the time of Vatican II, there was little cause to foresee the travels that the Holy Father Pope John Paul II would undertake during his papacy, which changed the episcopacy as well as the papacy. Put differently, conventional understandings of the local bishops' authority role (not to say authority itself?) were at least juxtaposed by the presence, preaching, and teaching of the Holy Father on these visits. Again, a possible question is whether the vision of ordained ministries in a diocese—bishop, presbyter, deacon—as envisioned in *Lumen Gentium* based on traditional sources can, in fact, be implemented with the increased importance and worldwide presence of the papacy, both physically and through the media.

64. See http://www.vatican.va/holy_father/benedict_xvi/homilies/2012/documents/hf_ben-xvi_hom_20120405_messa-crismale_en.html. My personal reaction was surprise that this was done in a homily just before the church was to enter the Triduum, the most sacred part of the liturgical year.

65. See http://www.vatican.va/holy_father/benedict_xvi/letters/2012/documents/hf_ben-xvi_let_20120414_zollitsch_en.html.

66. See Pope Paul VI, "Questa Udienza settimanale," *L'Osservatore Romano*, August 6, 1964; English translation, "The Idea of an Encyclical," *The Pope Speaks* 10 (1964–65): 248–51; also see Francis G. Morrisey, *The Canonical Significance of Papal and Curial Pronouncements* (Washington, DC: Canon Law Society of America, 1978), 2.

67. See Morrisey, *The Canonical Significance of Papal and Curial Pronouncements*, chapter 2, 21–22.

68. See *Dominicae Cenae*, n. 1, http://www.vatican.va/holy_father/john_paul_ii/letters/documents/hf_jp-ii_let_24021980_dominicae-cenae_en.html.

69. It is also noteworthy that, in the opinion of some scholars, the "certain aspects" of eucharistic theology and practice selected for comment correspond to the various criticisms leveled against the "new Mass" by Archbishop Marcel Lefebvre. See P.-M. Gy, "La lettre *Dominicae Cenae* sous le mystère et le culte de la sainte eucharistie," *La Maison Dieu* 141 (1980): 34.

70. See Kilmartin, *Church, Eucharist, and Priesthood*, 11.

71. From the *General Instruction of the Roman Missal*, n. 73:

The offerings are then brought forward. It is praiseworthy for the bread and wine to be presented by the faithful. They are then accepted at an appropriate place by the priest or the deacon and carried to the altar. Even though the faithful no longer bring from their own possessions the bread and wine intended for the liturgy as in the past, nevertheless the rite of carrying up the offerings still retains its force and its spiritual significance.

From http://www.usccb.org/prayer-and-worship/the-mass/general-instruction-of-the-roman-missal/. See George Nursey, "*Suscipe Munera Nostra*: A Liturgical Theology from the Prayers Over the Gifts for Sundays in Ordinary Time" (PhD dissertation, Catholic University of America, 2010).

72. See *Sacrosanctum Concilium*, n. 48; Pope Paul VI's 1974 *motu proprio* on Mass stipends entitled *Firma in Traditione*, accessible at http://www.vatican.va/holy_father/paul_vi/motu_proprio/documents/hf_p-vi_motu-proprio_19740613_firma-in-traditione_it.html; as well as Kilmartin, *Church, Eucharist, and Priesthood*, 66.

73. See Hans Urs von Balthasar, "The Mass, a Sacrifice of the Church?" in *Explorations in Theology* III: *Creator Spiritus* (San Francisco: Ignatius Press, 1993), 185–243.

74. Translation from Pope John Paul II, *Holy Thursday Letters to My Brother Priests* (Chicago: Midwest Theological Forum, 1994), 211.

75. In addition to his full-length monograph, see Paul Cordes's *Sendung zum Dienst. Exegetisch-historische und systematische Studien zum Konsilsdekret "Vom Dient und Leben der Priester"* (Frankfurt am Main: Josef Knecht, 1972), and his "*Sacerdos alter Christus?* Der

Repräsentationsgedanke in der Amtstheologie," *Catholica* 26, no. 1 (1972): 38–49.

76. In addition, see the brief but insightful article by James Puglisi, "Presider as *Alter Christus*: Head of the Body?" *Liturgical Ministry* 10 (Summer 2001): 153–58; as well as a pastoral-theological discussion about the relative merits of reviving the term today in Christopher Ruddy, *Tested in Every Way: The Catholic Priesthood in Today's Church* (New York: Herder and Herder, 2006), 49–104 (passim).

77. See, among others, the insightful summary of this term from within the Sulpician tradition and as reflected in his copious documentation, in Lawrence Terrien's "Living Sacraments: Some Reflections on Priesthood in Light of the French School and Documents of the Magisterium," in Terrien and others, *Ministerial Priesthood in the Third Millennium: Faithfulness of Christ, Faithfulness of Priests* (Collegeville, MN: Liturgical Press, 2009), 33–36, and fn. 11 and 15. Terrien asserts that for the Sulpician founder Jean Jacques Olier, the term *alter Christus* referred to the baptized and that it was only later appropriated in the Sulpician tradition to refer to the ordained in a fairly exalted way.

78. See http://www.vatican.va/holy_father/john_paul_ii/letters/2000/documents/hf_jp-ii_let_20000330_priests_en.html.

79. A consultant to an east coast diocesan personnel board stated fifteen years ago that this approach to restructuring "will kill a dying breed—priests."

80. The *Catechism* chapter titled "Sacraments at the Service of Communion" encompasses both holy orders and matrimony. *The Catechism of the Catholic Church* (Washington, DC: United States Catholic Conference, 1994), nn. 1533–1666. The material just on holy orders is from numbers 1533 to 1600.

81. See S. Bonaventurae, *Opera Theologica Selecta*, ed. Pacifici M. Perantoni, tomus IV, liber IV, Sententiarum, "De Sacramentis et Novissimus" (Firenze: Quaracchi, 1949), 594–649, at 608–17.

82. Aquinas, *Summa Theologiae*, III a, q. 63, arts. 1–6, q. 65, art. 3, and q. 72, art. 5. That he described baptism as a "passive power" and confirmation as a "spiritual battle" is of interest, and is dealt with carefully and thoroughly by Colman O'Neill, in "The Role of the Recipient and Sacramental Signification," published in two parts in *The Thomist* 31 (July 1958): 257–301 and *The Thomist* 31 (October 1958): 508–40.

83. Sullivan, *Creative Fidelity*, 17.

84. See the *Summa Theologiae* III, q. 63, arts 1, 2c, q. 72, art. 5, q. 80, art. 10. See Piet Fransen, "The Sacramental Character at the Council of Trent," *Bijdragen* 32 (1971): 2–33.

85. Despite the useful summary of magisterial assertions about the priestly character in David Toups, *Reclaiming Priestly Character* (Omaha: The Institute for Priestly Formation, 2008), the rest of this work is more anecdotal than insightful.

86. All translations are from http://www.vatican.va/holy_father/john_paul_ii/apost_exhortations/documents/hf_jp-ii_exh_25031992_pastores-dabo-vobis_en.html.

87. See http://www.vatican.va/holy_father/paul_vi/encyclicals/documents/hf_p-vi_enc_24061967_sacerdotalis_en.html, esp. nn. 26, 28, 33.

88. See http://www.vatican.va/roman_curia/congregations/cfaith/documents/rc_con_cfaith_doc_19761015_inter-insigniores_en.html, n 5.

89. On the nature of this document see, among others, the afore-mentioned texts of Sullivan and Morrissey, as well as Sara Butler, *The Catholic Priesthood and Women: A Guide to the Teaching of the Church* (Chicago/Mundelein: Hillenbrand Books, 2006), 2, 15–17. In the same book, on the pope's use of spousal imagery, see 80–90. With regard to the *Responsum ad Dubium* issued by the Congregation of the Doctrine of the Faith, see Richard Gaillardetz, "Infallibility and the Ordination of Women," *Louvain Studies* 21 (1995): 3–24, especially 6–7 and the important bibliographical references in fn. 8, where Gaillardetz cites Francis Sullivan, who asserted that "the most significant aspect of *Ordinatio Sacerdotalis* was that it appeared to presume a new category of magisterial teaching, an exercise of the ordinary papal magisterium which could propose teaching to be held as definitive and irreformable," taken from Sullivan's own statements in "New Claims for the Pope," *The Tablet* 18 (June 18, 1994): 768.

90. Among others, see David Bohr, "The Spousal Meaning of Celibacy," in *The Diocesan Priest: Consecrated and Sent* (Collegeville, MN: Liturgical Press, 2009), 124–57.

91. These aspects of priestly ministry and priestly spirituality should be recalled when trying to delineate a proper (diocesan) priest's spirituality. See my own "A Spirituality for the Priest: Apostolic, Relational, Liturgical," in Terrien and others, *Ministerial Priesthood in the Third Millennium*, 86–107. One of my critiques of the recently pub-

lished study by Stephen J. Rossetti, *Why Priests Are Happy: A Study of the Psychological and Spiritual Health of Priests* (Notre Dame, IN: Ave Maria Press, 2011), is that no questions were asked about the place of the celebration of the Eucharist in the life of the priest. In addition, despite its popularity, I find the thesis and contents of George Aschenbrenner's *Quickening the Fire in Our Midst: The Challenge of Diocesan Priestly Spirituality* (Chicago: Loyola Press, 2002) more of an application of certain aspects of a Jesuit approach to spirituality rather than one suited to the diocesan priest. In addition I judge the treatment of liturgy and sacraments as not reflective of a postconciliar vision based on full, conscious, and active participation presided over by the priest whose very presidency requires skills and spiritual talents not addressed here.

92. See http://www.vatican.va/edocs/ENG0821/_INDEX.HTM.

93. See http://www.vatican.va/holy_father/benedict_xvi/apost_ex hortations/documents/hf_ben-xvi_exh_20070222_sacramentum-cari tatis_en.html.

94. See http://www.vatican.va/holy_father/benedict_xvi/apost_ex hortations/documents/hf_ben-xvi_exh_20100930_verbum-domini _en.html.

CHAPTER FOUR

1. Avery Dulles, *The Priestly Life: A Theological Reflection* (New York/Mahwah, NJ: Paulist Press, 1997), 11.

2. See Robert Kaslyn, *"Communion with the Church" and the Code of Canon Law: An Analysis of the Foundation and Implications of the Canonical Obligation to Maintain Communion with the Catholic Church* (Lewiston, NY: Edwin Mellen Press, 1994).

3. The history of what oil was used for ordinations and when it was used is a complex historical and liturgical study (particularly in Carolingian sources). See Gerard Ellard, *Ordination Anointings in the Western Church Before 1000 A.D.* (Cambridge, MA: The Medieval Academy of America, 1970). For the pre–Vatican II rite see, among others, *The Rite of Ordination According to the Roman Pontifical* (New York: The Cathedral Library Association, 1924), 64.

4. I regard the work by Bernard-Dominique Marliangeas, *Clés pour une théologie du ministère. In Persona Christi, In Persona Ecclesiae* (Paris: Editions Beauchesne, 1978), as something of a classic. See also Mary Schaefer, "'In Persona Christi': Cult of the Priest's Person or Active Presence of Christ?" in *In God's Hands: Essays in Honor of Michael A. Fahey*, ed. Jaroslav Z. Skira and Michael S. Attridge, 77–201 (Leuven: University Press, 2006).

5. See *Sacrae Disciplinae Leges*, in *Codex Iuris Canonici* 83.

6. Among others, see H. Rokhof, "The Competence of Priests, Prophets and Kings: Ecclesiological Reflections about the Power and Authority of Christian Believers," *Concilium* 197, no. 3 (1988): 53–62.

7. See V. De Paolis, "*Communio* in novo CIC," *Periodica de re morali, canonica, liturgica* 7 (1988): 521–52, at 523.

8. See R. Castillo Lara, "La communion ecclésiale dans le nouveau Code de droit canonique," *Studia Canonica* 17 (1983): 224–45, at 241: in a strict sense, "hierarchical communion represents the organic and structural level which binds members of the hierarchy among themselves, especially within the episcopal college, but it equally embraces their relationships with their priests as well as their relationships with their deacons."

9. See Robert J. Kaslyn, "*Communion with the Church" and the Code of Canon Law.*

10. Ibid., 140.

11. See, among others, Paul Hennessy, ed., *A Concert of Charisms: Ordained Ministry in Religious Life* (New York/Mahwah, NJ: Paulist Press, 1997); and John Burkhard, "Presbyteral Identity Today," *New Theology Review* 17, no. 2 (August 2004): 19–29.

12. For example, see Dean R. Hoge, *The First Five Years of the Priesthood: A Study of Newly Ordained Catholic Priests* (Collegeville, MN: Liturgical Press, 2002); and Dean R. Hoge, *Experiences of Priests Ordained Five to Nine Years* (Collegeville, MN: Liturgical Press, 2006). This is not to assert, however, that the Hoge research is beyond critique. A real problem is the requirement that respondents have to choose between two "models" delineated by James Bacik in "The Practice of Priesthood: Working Through Today's Tensions," in Karen Sue Smith, ed., *Priesthood in the Modern World* (Franklin, WI: Sheed and Ward, 1999), 54–65: "the cultic model" and "the servant-leader model." See Hoge, *Experiences of Priests Ordained Five to Nine Years*,

59–71. This is to separate the inseparable and to fall into an either/or, not to say caricatured, approach to the admittedly complex theology of orders.

13. See the recently published *Same Call, Different Men: The Evolution of the Priesthood since Vatican II,* ed. Mary Gautier, Paul Perl, and Stephen Fichter (Collegeville, MN: Liturgical Press, 2012).

14. See Hervé Marie Legrand, "The Presidency of the Eucharist according to the Ancient Tradition," in *Living Bread, Saving Cup,* ed. Kevin Seasoltz, 196–210 (Collegeville, MN: Liturgical Press, 1987).

15. See, among others, the insightful arguments made throughout Vincent Miller's *Consuming Religion: Christian Faith and Practice in a Consumer Culture* (New York: Continuum, 2003).

Select Bibliography

EUCHARIST

NEW TESTAMENT

Kodell, Jerome. *The Eucharist in the New Testament.* Wilmington, DE: Michael Glazier, 1988; now published by Liturgical Press. An enormously insightful commentary on the key texts in the New Testament about the Eucharist. Modest in size and inviting in writing style.

Leon-Dufour, Xavier. *Sharing the Eucharistic Bread: The Witness of the New Testament.* Translated by Matthew J. O'Connell. New York/Mahwah, NJ: Paulist Press, 1987; original French, 1982. A contemporary classic that is regrettably out of print. Gives the most careful and thorough analyses (diachronic and synchronic) of the New Testament. Worth the effort to study carefully.

PATRISTIC ERA

Jasper, R., and G. Cuming, eds. *Prayers of the Eucharist: Early and Reformed.* 2nd edition. A Pueblo Book. Collegeville, MN: Liturgical Press, 1990. An excellent commentary on the evolution and contents of the Eucharistic Prayer. Contains all the important texts of the Eucharistic Prayers, both Eastern and Western, starting from Jewish table prayers through the prayers from the reformed traditions.

MEDIEVAL ERA

Mitchell, Nathan. *Cult and Controversy: The Worship of the Eucharist Outside Mass.* New York: Pueblo Pub. Co., 1982. See part 1,

145

"History of the Cult of the Eucharist Outside Mass," 10–198. The best account of the evolution of eucharistic theology and practice from the patristic through the medieval periods. Very engagingly written and copiously documented.

Thomas Aquinas. *Summa Theologiae* III, qq, 73, 75, 76, 83.

Bonaventure, *Breviloquium* VI, 9.

These are classic texts, worth the effort to study both carefully for those with theological and historical background.

COUNCIL OF TRENT

Tanner, Norman P., ed. *Decrees of the Ecumenical Councils.* Vol. 2, *Trent to Vatican II.* Washington, DC: Georgetown University Press, 1990. See pages 693–98 and 732–37 for the Council of Trent's Decrees on the Sacrament and on the Sacrifice (available in both Latin and English). This is an indispensable starting point for a consideration of what the fathers at Trent decreed.

Tanner, Norman. "The Eucharist in the Ecumenical Councils." *Gregorianum* 82, no. 1 (2001): 37–49. A very important summary of the magisterium on the Eucharist from the patristic through the medieval periods.

CONTEMPORARY

In addition to the texts cited in the text:

Institutio Generalis Missale Romanum (General Instruction of the Roman Missal). Revised edition. Contains the protocols for the present Order of Mass with important (if pithy) theological explanations.

Irwin, Kevin. *Models of the Eucharist.* New York/Mahwah, NJ: Paulist Press, 2005. A distillation of ten ways to approach the theology and practice of the Eucharist drawn from liturgical sources and magisterial texts.

Von Balthasar, Hans Urs. *Explorations in Theology.* Vol. 3, *Creator Spirit.* San Francisco: Ignatius Press, 1993. See pages 185–243 for the chapter "The Mass, a Sacrifice of the Church?" An insightful and in-depth consideration of the Eucharist emphasizing memorial and ecclesiology.

ORDAINED PRIESTHOOD

NEW TESTAMENT

Sullivan, Francis. *From Apostles to Bishops: The Development of the Episcopacy in the Early Church*. Mahwah, NJ/New York: Newman, 2001. Perhaps among the most complex issues to be dealt with is the New Testament foundation for ordained priesthood. This book is stellar and, while focused on the episcopacy, it also tracks the evolution toward ordained priesthood in a highly informed way in chapters 1 to 3.

PATRISTIC ERA

Sullivan, Francis. *From Apostles to Bishops: The Development of the Episcopacy in the Early Church*. Mahwah, NJ/New York: Newman, 2001. The remaining chapters, 4 to 10, of this stellar book focus on the episcopacy with admirable clarity and insight.

Bradshaw, Paul. *Ordination Rites of the Ancient Churches*. Collegeville, MN: Liturgical Press, 1990. A collection of all major ordination rites in the East and West with helpful introductions.

Legrand, Hervé-Marie. "The Presidency of the Eucharist according to the Ancient Tradition." In *Living Bread, Saving Cup*, edited by Kevin Seasoltz, 196–21. Collegeville, MN: Liturgical Press, 1987. A veritable classic summary of the principle that one who oversees the church presides for the church.

MEDIEVAL PERIOD

Osborne, Kenan B. *Priesthood: A History of the Ordained Ministry in the Catholic Church*. New York/Mahwah, NJ: Paulist Press, 2003. See especially pages 89 to 129 and 200 to 18. An enormously insightful overview of the period. Unfortunately out of print.

Power, David N. *Ministers of Christ and His Church: The Theology of Priesthood*. London: Geoffrey Chapman, 1969. Pages 113 to 126 provide a brief but very useful overview of a complex period, theologically nuanced and carefully presented.

CONTEMPORARY PERIOD

Dulles, Avery. *The Priestly Office: A Theological Reflection.* New York/Mahwah, NJ: Paulist Press, 1997. A highly readable summary of key insights from the magisterium on priesthood.

Kasper, Walter Cardinal. *Leadership in the Church.* New York: Herder & Herder, 2003. Chapters 1 to 4 are theologically and historically grounded essays on the diaconate, the priestly office, the episcopal office, and apostolic succession.

Ministerial Priesthood in the Third Millennium: Faithfulness of Christ, Faithfulness of Priests. Collegeville, MN: Liturgical Press, 2009. This book contains five essays from the symposium held at The Catholic University of America for the Year of Priests:

1. Ronald D. Witherup, "The Biblical Foundations of Priesthood: The Contributions of the Letter to the Hebrews," 1–23.
2. Lawrence B. Terrien, "Living Sacraments: Some Reflections on Priesthood in Light of the French School and Documents of the Magisterium," 24–42.
3. Michael J. Witczak, "Faithful Stewards of God's Mysteries: Theological Insights on Priesthood from the Ordination Ritual," 43–60.
4. Paul J. McPartlan, "Priesthood, Priestliness, and Priests," 61–85.
5. Kevin W. Irwin, "A Spirituality for the Priest: Apostolic, Relational, Liturgical," 86–107.